DOMAINS

OF

DECISION

MANAGEMENT

DOMAINS

OF

DECISION

MANAGEMENT

MANAGEMENT INNOVATION FOR
HIGHER-QUALITY DECISIONS

JAMES E. MOFFETT, SR.

Domains of Decision Management: Management Innovation for Higher-Quality Decisions

Published by Wheatmark˚
2030 East Speedway Boulevard, Suite 106
Tucson, Arizona 85719 USA
www.wheatmark.com

ISBN: 978-1-62787-749-7 (paperback)
ISBN: 978-1-62787-750-3 (ebook)
LCCN: 2019912806

Bulk ordering discounts are available through Wheatmark, Inc. For more information, email orders@wheatmark.com or call 1-888-934-0888.

rev202101

Dedication

This sincere effort to assist managers and all decision-makers is dedicated to Mama Pheobe F. Moffett and Dad London Moffett Jr., both long-time Mississippi educators, and to my wife Frances L. Moffett and our son James E. Moffett, Jr.

The decision guidance in this book is sincere and offered to leaders and managers of all levels. Leaders are responsible for directing our most prominent corporations, mid-sized companies, and our smallest Main Street stores. The one common factor among them all is the leadership's responsibility to make well-considered decisions. That is the purpose of this book, to present a decision-making process that considers the firm's people, the time element, the financials, the organization, and moral and ethical considerations. Learning this process will help leaders and managers understand decisions and make "Decisions with Principles."

Contents

List of Figures

List of Tables

Acknowledgements

Sincere appreciation goes to several dedicated professionals who offered their quality experiences to this research project. The research purpose entailed seeking an improved method to combat the effects of decision distractions, barriers, impediments, and thinking detours that often lead well-intended managers to acquiesce, to satisfice, and to settle for short-cut heuristics rather than adhering to a well-defined and structured decision process. The Domains of Decision Management (DDM) offers beleaguered managers something new, a management innovation complete with defined steps to higher-quality decisions.

Those offering their professional expertise included Frances L. Moffett, wife; Dr. Glenn Simmons, Dr. Kathleen Bullock, and Dr. Angelica Landry, Wayland Baptist University, Sierra Vista, AZ Campus; Chaplain (MAJ) Yan Xiong, Fort Huachuca, AZ; and Dr. Becky Dorman and Regina Massich, Cochise College, Sierra Vista, AZ.

Again, thank you for your support, management thoughts, and technical expertise.

Preface

The roots of the Domains of Decision Management (DDM) research began in 1978. At that time, I was serving my country as a US Army captain in central Germany. As a unit commander of a tactical signal company, I learned to appreciate and respect people, correctly, the 125 men and women in the unit.

One Army tradition that probably will never end is a Command Inspection. In that dreaded inspection, five critical unit tasks were on the list. Failing any one unit task could be the difference between a successful command experience and an unsuccessful one.

One crucial unit task is Supply. You know, the process of identifying, ordering, receiving, distributing, and accounting for every single item. It is a monumental undertaking. Approximately three weeks before the inspection day, the unit Supply Sergeant (E6) passed away. With only a Specialist Fourth Class to fill his shoes, the perceived inspection outcome was questionable.

However, with personnel assistance from another unit and, most of all, the US Armed Forces Recreation Center (AFRC) in southern Germany, and daily motivational orations to the soldiers, I believed the company could be successful. It worked. The company passed all five tasks. The following Sunday morning three tour busses arrived at the unit, loaded many of the soldiers and their families for four-to-five days relaxation and fun activities.

How was a Command Inspection associated with a research project 42 years later?

First, I learned people matter. I learned being open and fair made a difference. Being considerate, that is, respecting others, and attending to their needs mattered. Moreover, taking care of the soldiers encouraged them to take care of that unit inspection.

Next, I learned timing mattered. No time was lost, informing the unit about the loss of our well-liked Supply Sergeant. Formulating Plan B became a top priority. The First Sergeant agreed an AFRC trip may work. There was no time lost in coordinating the AFRC accommodations for the soldiers. In this case, time was a friend.

Third, I learned and coordinated the transport and distribution of unit pay (i.e., financials) to the soldiers far away from home. Imagine not paying 100 soldiers on time. Paid soldiers were happy soldiers.

Fourth, I learned to balance the obligation to the soldiers and responsibility to the unit (or organization). The unit passed the inspection because motivated soldiers could imagine and see vacation fun following the inspection. I now know I was practicing path-goal leadership.

Last, it was the ethical thing to do. It is recognizing and living up to obligations and motivating the workforce. Speaking well of an excellent departed soldier, and placing the soldiers' wellbeing above my own. That is what ethical leaders do.

It is ironic these five entities – people, time, financials, the organization, and moral and ethical concerns – are so prevalent and relevant in today's organizations. While much has changed in 42 years, much has remained the same, especially when making ethical decisions may change peoples' lives.

Researchers Sekaran and Bougie (2016) began their book, *Research Methods for Business*, by conveying, "The difference between making good decisions and committing blunders often lies in how we go about the decision-making process" (p. 2). Decision blunders may be groupthink, hasty decisions, financial egoism, garbage-can thinking, governance failures, a paradox of choice, and bounded rationality, to name a few.

This writing is a plain-language journey into an epoch of higher-quality decisions. A process that keeps senior managers involved. It is a prescriptive approach complete with structured steps. DDM is an opportunity for managers and followers to contribute very beneficial decisions to organization success.

The Domains of Decision Management is innovative because of its convergence of senior management responsibility and oversight; having a repetitive process; being systematic and structured; having objective and subjective components; and five independent and interdependent Domains: *people, time, financials, the organization,* and *moral* and *ethical concerns.*

Also, DDM has operational mediating variables: evaluating, questioning, and researching, and process mediating variables: proactive communications, integration, coordination, and collaboration. DDM's most significant perpetual quality is its institutionalization as a management innovation. In other words, leaders should instill the mantra "DDM: Decisions with principles."

The original unpublished DDM theory paper was submitted for US Copyright Office registration circa December 31, 2016. It was titled: *Domains of Decision Management: A Treatise in the Methodology of Managerial Decision Making.* That document was approved for registration on July 25, 2017. This writing presents the DDM research, as well as case study research seeking a better understanding of Wells Fargo and Volkswagen likely decision factors. These studies conclude offering comprehensive recommendations to organization leaders committed to higher-quality decisions and improved organizational performance.

According to Hal Urban in his book, *Life's Greatest Lessons: 20 Things That Matter,* "What we become depends not on conditions but on decisions" (2003, p. 14). The researcher agrees with this conviction, which in large part applies to organization managers as well.

James E. Moffett, Sr.
Sierra Vista, AZ 2019

Research Summary

How executives perceive a decision environment and make decisions may have contributed to recent problematic decisions costing Wells Fargo* at least $185 million, and Volkswagen* more than $30 billion (Egan, 2016; Ewing, 2019; Glazer, 2016a). In the Wells Fargo *cross-sales* case, approximately 5,300 employees and about three dozen District Managers lost their jobs (Calabresi, 2016; Glazer, 2018). The Volkswagen *clean-diesel* case was described as being worse than Enron* (Bach, 2015). These problematic decisions were the impetus for this collective case study (CCS). Eight research questions ranged from what kinds of actions describe this collective case study, to what the five most likely factors are for the Wells Fargo and Volkswagen decisions. This dual-purpose study also tested an innovative prescriptive decision theory that "managers may achieve very beneficial and advantageous decisions by systematically evaluating five interdependent management Domains – people, time, financials, the organization, and moral and ethical implications." The study employed traditional case study, qualitative, and quantitative procedures, including Domains of Decision Management (DDM) respondents and separate combined CCS Wells Fargo and Volkswagen respondents. Data analysis produced 45-plus total DDM and CCS themes. Ninety-one percent of respondents believed the DDM theory possessed the potential to produce above-average to very beneficial decisions. The Pearson's *r* correlation coefficient measured a strong, positive 0.96. Case similarities, differences, and analytic generalizations surfaced. Innovative study recommendations included *Golden Rule*-type decisions. Wells Fargo and VW appear to appreciate decision learning – both are undergoing major management reorganizations. Very beneficial decisions are possible, provided ethically-minded managers embrace a structured, objective, subjective, and institutionalized decision process, which DDM purports to provide.

Key words: Leadership, Management, Rational decisions, Prescriptive decisions, Wells Fargo, Cross-sales, Volkswagen, Clean-diesel

1 The Problem, Wells Fargo, Volkswagen, and Why?

Decisions have consequences. Sekaran and Bougie assert, "The difference between making good decisions and committing blunders often lies in how we go about the decision-making process" (2016, p. 2). A problem. Managers are encouraged to re-think their decision-making purpose and process to avoid decision blunders and to make a reasoned choice to higher-quality decisions. The Domains of Decision Management (DDM) is an opportunity for managers to change their thinking and explore this new and innovative decision-making process.

Wells Fargo and Cross-Selling

When decision-makers fail to evaluate, question, and research decision consequences, decision implementation may become problematic. Such was arguably the case for Wells Fargo.

The company management and employees' questionable conduct appears to have dated back to 2002 (Back, 2016; Calabresi, 2016; Glazer, 2017b, c). Senior Wells Fargo executives endorsed the cross-selling practice, as did the CEO. The CEO in a 2010 annual report exclaimed, "Perhaps our new cheer should be 'Let's go again for ten'" (Glazer, 2016b, p. A8), referring to increasing the cross-selling goal to ten products per customer (Glazer, 2016a, 2017c). Wells

Fargo, operating within an unethical culture, appeared to have maximized bank revenue and the unethical impact on the banks' internal employees and 2.1 million external customers (Carucci, 2016; Johnson & McCoy, 2016; Witman, 2018). Later, the affected customers increased to 3.5 million (Glazer 2017b). When US regulators uncovered the cross-selling and employee blackballing that permanently barred employees from future banking employment, punitive action was warranted. The bank was fined $185 million (Cowley, 2016; Glazer, 2017c). Over 5,300 employees lost their jobs for being complicit in the scandal or resigned because of ethical dissonance, and recently, about three dozen District Managers were released (Burchard, 2011; Egan, 2016; Glazer, 2018). Subsequently, the CEO, who tolerated questionable employee conduct and weak governance, retired (Krantz, 2016). In an unprecedented action, the Board of Directors was ordered by federal regulators to replace four of its members (Elson & Ingram, 2018), and bank assets could not exceed $2 trillion (Flitter, Appelbaum, & Enrich, 2018). When decision-makers fail to envision decision outcomes, problems may arise.

Wells Fargo's culture has been described as unethical, reprehensible, a pressure-cooker environment, and "wholly inconsistent with the values on which Wells Fargo was built"... "Spiraling out of control," describes the cross-sells activity by a 2005 corporate investigating manager (Carucci, 2016; Eisen, 2020, pp. A1, A10). That said, see the company revenue (in billions) and Fortune 500 rankings below:

- 2011: 26th, $87.597B

- 2012: 26th, $91.247B

- 2013: 25th, $88.069B

- 2014: 29th, $88.372B

- 2015: 30th, $90.033B

- 2016: 27th, $94.176B

- 2017: 25th, $97.741B

- 2018: 26th, $101.060B

- 2019: 29th, $103.915B (Fortune.com 500; Macrotrends.net, 2020).

The above characterizations of Wells Fargo's culture are alarming and regrettable. One has to wonder how the Bank's culture transformed itself from strong and upstanding to unethical and reprehensible – a dismal predicament. Such a culture points out how managers must remain alert and protective of an ethical organizational culture. However, without committed managers, it will not happen.

Maintaining a strong ethical culture is not easy, especially when the leaders do not sell the culture and its benefits to all. The culture must be communicated and sold. One method of selling an ethical culture is recurring company training that is fun. It works. Well planned purposeful role-play having *three points to remember* makes a difference. Three points may be: 1) Improves the company reputation, 2) Lessens company compliance issues, and 3) Reduces the pressure of an unethical environment.

From the evidence, Wells Fargo managers have learned an indelible lesson about decisions and decision learning. Decision learning, in this case, means learning from previous less successful decisions (Daft, 2016) and applying that knowledge toward more ethical and sustainable business practices (Gamble, Peteraf, & Thompson, 2017). For Wells Fargo, sustainable business practices refer to aggressively enacting and enforcing policies and procedures sufficient for today's employees, customers, and stakeholders' needs, without jeopardizing the needs of future employees, customers, and stakeholders.

Volkswagen and Clean-Diesel

Automakers are formidable competitors. In 2006, Mercedes introduced an environmentally friendly clean-diesel. Mercedes-Benz, VW, and Audi agreed to share the new emissions technology to increase their collective clean-diesel sells. However, because of VW's engineering pride and arrogance, VW developed its own clean-diesel; it was not successful (Mahler, 2015). A problematic decision resulted from VW's effort. The Volkswagen clean-diesel included vehicle software programmed, purposely, to pass random auto emission tests (Ewing & Mouawad, 2015). Further, VW received multiple environmental awards for its clean-diesel innovation (Gates et al., 2015). The vehicle software reverted to a performance state of excessive and illegal vehicle emission levels. These unethical and deliberate decisions cost VW more than $30 billion and Bosch, writer of the software, $327.5 million (Boston, 2018; Ewing, 2017a, b; Ewing, 2019). US regulators learned about the emission tests in 2014 from West Virginia University, the testing site. Brooks and Dunn (2018) asserted: "It is evident that many VW employees and managers knew of this illegal deception of cheating on emissions standards from 2009 to 2014, thus putting the company at great financial and reputational risk" (p. 144). McGee and Storbeck (2019), in Frankfort, Germany, declared the deception occurred from 2006 to 2015. That is even more surprising.

Legal issues abound. Gates et al. reported that VW's top management was uninformed about the planned deception (2015). The then VW CEO resigned (Hakim, Kessler, & Ewing, 2015). German prosecutors formally charged that CEO, April 2019, with aggravated fraud, infringement of competition law, and embezzlement. Prosecutors argued the CEO failed to alert responsible authorities in Germany and the US about the illegal emission devices. If convicted, he faces a jail term of six months to 10 years (McGee & Storbeck, 2019). The former Audi Chief Executive and three others were arrested and charged with fraud in the clean-diesel deception (Bomey, 2018; Eddy, 2019). Audi is a VW subsidiary. Also, German prosecutors for negligent violation of supervisory duties named Porsche as enabling the clean-diesel deception (McGee, 2019b), and was fined 535 million Euros. Porsche is a VW subsidiary.

The Volkswagen Accountability Project (VAP) advocacy group broadcasted that VW's corrupt culture reintroduced thousands of emission deficient vehicles back to the market (VAP, 2018). Owners of these vehicles may well have perceived their particular vehicle as being counterfeit – a VW betrayal. Such perceptions are accurate, according to Amar, Ariely, Carmon, and Yang (2018), who researched the effects of counterfeit products. They found there is a moral disgust for known counterfeit products and genuine products having the same label. Regarding the VAP allegation, the researcher interviews with VW Sales Managers found a valid business model to buy back, repair, and sell the upgraded vehicles as Certified VW used cars.

VW's buybacks of diesel automobiles are ahead of schedule (Roberts, 2017), and VW has settled its State of Arizona lawsuit for $40 million (Fischer, 2018). Now, BMW is facing a potential $1 billion fine for collusion in the deception (Boston & Norman, 2019). European authorities appear to take these offenses more severely than American authorities do.

Volkswagen acknowledged its authoritarian leadership and toxic culture (Ewing, 2019, p. 3) that resulted in a mission culture stressing high performance, high-level competitiveness (win-at-all-costs), and a profit-making orientation (Daft, 2016; Quinn, 1988). VW's competition with Toyota for world leader has been a top priority for years. See the VW Global 500 rankings and the VW annual revenues, in billions, from 2006 to 2019 below. Clean diesel (CD):

- 2006: 17th, $118B (Behind Toyota)

- 2007: 18th, $149B (Behind Toyota)

- 2008: 8th, $149B (Behind Toyota)

- 2009: 14th, $167B (Behind Toyota)

- 2010: 16th, $146B (Behind Toyota)

- 2011: 13th, $168B (Behind Toyota)

- 2012: 12th, $221B (Behind Toyota)

- 2013: 9th, $248B (Behind Toyota)

- 2014: 8th, $261B (Year of CD disclosure) (Topped Toyota)

- 2015: 8th, $268B (Topped Toyota)

- 2016: 7th, $238B (Topped Toyota)

- 2017: 6th, $240B (Behind Toyota)

- 2018: 7th, $260B (Behind Toyota)

- 2019: 9th, $278B (Topped Toyota) (Fortune Global 500).

The CD deception reportedly began in 2006; VW revenues increased substantially from 2006 to 2014. Perhaps a manager (having knowledge of the deception) argued the VW revenues are good, very good, why change the business model? From 2015 to 2019 VW's revenue average was $256.8B. Any revenue decline from the CD vehicles was covered by VW's 12-plus other brands (Volkswagen AG, 2020). This revenue decline possibly reflects the public and stock market clean-diesel reaction.

VW's efforts were clearly focused on short-term profits and not focused on the long-term health of the company's brand, its employees, or the environment, as analyzed by Bansal, King, and Seijts (2015/ 2018).

Bach's (2015) article, "Seven Reasons VW is Worse than Enron," makes apparent how malicious VW's deliberate fraud was. While the Enron fraud eliminated the savings of thousands of employees, VW's illegal nitrogen oxide emissions endangered the lives of millions of Americans. Enron's bankruptcy cost approximately $2.6 billion, while VW costs have exceeded $30 billion (McGee, 2019a). Two reasons the Enron case was small compared to VW.

When managers fail to learn from previous decisions and do not evaluate, question, and research decision consequences, decision implementation may become problematic. It appears that VW managers have learned an unforgettable lesson to accept nothing less than more ethical and sustainable business practices (Gamble, Peteraf, & Thompson, 2017). Somewhat similar to Wells Fargo, sustainable business practices refer to being proactive enacting and enforcing policies and procedures sufficient for today's employees, customers, and stakeholders' needs, without jeopardizing the needs of future employees, customers, and stakeholders. Further, to compete honestly in the automotive marketplace.

Why Problematic Decisions?

Were the Wells Fargo and Volkswagen decisions satisficed (Simon, 1997)? Possibly, a paradox of choice baffled the executives (Kida, Moreno, & Smith, 2010). Did information-short quasirationality contribute (Hammond, 2010)? Were these garbage-can decisions (Cohen, March, & Olsen, 1972)? Perhaps both cases were greed induced as argued in the ethical counterviews (Verschool, 2002). Corporate governance failures (Ewing & Mouawad, 2015; Carucci, 2016)? Were menacing ethical blind spots at work (Werhane et al., 2014)? Moreover, did social science-related factors influence the decisions: ethical dissonance, groupthink, and inherited decisions (Burchard, 2011; Festinger, 1957; Janis, 1982)? Was there a strong devil's advocate present? Did Wells Fargo and VW possess excessive influence-rich decision environments? Were there unethical and toxic cultures (Ewing, 2019)?

A Kuhnian paradigm shift in executive decision thinking was overdue (Kuhn, 1970). These problematic decisions together with employee and customer hardships underscored the need for a collective case study (CCS), and an examination of a more systematic, structured, objective, subjective, and institutionalized approach to higher-quality managerial decisions. Accordingly, the Domains of Decision Management Model (DDM) is theorized.

2 Opportunity, Objectives, Domains, and Benefits

Opportunity refers to a significant favorable situation in a firm's environment (Pearce & Robinson, 2013). That opportunity is "The Domains of Decision Management (DDM), a prescriptive decision-making model, that posits managers may achieve very beneficial decisions by systematically evaluating five interdependent management Domains – people, time, financials, the organization, and moral and ethical implications." Currently, a high-quality decision, according to Chevron Corporation's* decision researchers, refers to "the course of action that will capture the most value, given the uncertainties and complexities of the real world (Neal & Spetzler, 2015)." DDM argues that opportunities exist for managers to make very beneficial and advantageous decisions.

This research has demonstrated, theoretically, that a very beneficial decision is possible. One Peer Debriefer questioned the term *very*. She argued, rightfully so, that very was not quantifiable. It is noted that decision theory harbors several non-quantifiable terms. For example, *optimal* means most favorable, *perfect* means being without fault or defect, and *effective* means producing a strong or desired effect. *Very* means extremely, incredible, and exceptional. It appears non-quantifiable decision theorists are content having a collection of qualitative-related terms. Therefore, for now, very beneficial will remain a qualitative descriptor of DDM capabilities.

Executives desiring more consistent, higher-quality decisions should subscribe to DDM's philosophy, transform their decision thinking, and benefit from DDM's institutionalization as a management innovation.

DDM and CCS Protocol Research Objectives (RO)

The DDM and collective case study *research objectives* were:
RO1. To describe what this collective case study is about
RO2. To describe the collective case study similarities
RO3. To describe the collective case study differences
RO4. To describe the collective case study analytic generalizations
RO5. To describe likely factors influencing specific Wells Fargo and Volkswagen executive decisions. *Factor* refers to "a circumstance, fact, or influence that helps to bring about a result" (Hawker, 2006, p. 246).

RO6. To evaluate the DDM prescriptive theory that "managers may achieve very beneficial and advantageous decisions by systematically evaluating five interdependent management Domains – people, time, financials, the organization, and moral and ethical implications."

Worldview, discussed later, and research objectives guided the theoretical perspectives, the sample, data collection, and analysis. Remaining focused on these objectives creates the opportunity for managers to develop sustainable business practices.

Nature of the Domains

The Domains are specified spheres of activity, interest, and knowledge (Hawker, 2006). See Table 1. First, *people* constitute the organization's human and intellectual capital. People working with tacit and explicit knowledge communicate quantitative and qualitative data creating valuable competitive advantages (Smith & Flanagan, 2006). Second, *time* is the finite, irreplaceable opportunity resource in which organizations achieve goals; time may be friend or foe. Third, *financials* represent economic position and performance (Drucker, 2001). Fourth, *organizations*, originally defined here as purposeful entities

Table 1 Domains of Decision Management©	
Domains	Nature of the Domains
People	Competitive advantage
Time	An opportunity resource
Financials	Economic performance
The Organization	Ultimate unit of success
Morals and Ethics	How should we live?

of employees, resources, management, and leadership, may be sole proprietorships or global corporations, as in the *Fortune* 500 (Chew, Griffith, Hackett, Kowitt, Lev-Ram, Lorenzetti, Marinova, Primack, & Rao, 2016; DeCarlo, & Rapp, 2016). Fifth, in this post-Enron and Bernard Madoff era, managers should afford particular attention to operational transparency and addressing *moral* and *ethical* issues (Maglich, 2013; Segal, 2018; Smith, 2009). The five Domains are core DDM tenets.

The five Domains are interdependent because of the symbiotic and resource-dependent relationships existing among them. Indeed, if any Domain receives less than maximum collective work effort, it may cause irreparable harm to the remaining Domains. Maximum collective work effort refers to each working individual exerting his or her maximum effort either continuously or over a series of separate work periods. Carmody's (2011) continuous work or a series of work periods allows sports players and employees to exceed the 100% barrier. DDM responsible managers and employees must be committed to the DDM process and to exceeding their personal limits.

Benefits of DDM Research to People and Organizations

Occasionally managers exhibit authentic concern for employees. The 1940's Behavioral approach to management introduced the constructs of *consideration* and *initiating structure*. Consideration behaviors include mutual respect, trust, and friendship (Stogdill, & Coons, 1957). Three excellent examples of consideration and its consequences in the corporate world are Google,® Wegmans® Food Market, and AT&T.®

Arguably, Google, Wegmans Food Markets, and AT&T would not be as successful without executives making judicious business and people-oriented decisions. Several common characteristics of these companies have been knowledgeable decision-makers, recognition, and consideration for employees. In *Fortune*'s 2016 "Best 100 Companies to Work For," Google rated Number One and Wegmans Number Four; in 2017, Google rated Number One, and Wegmans rated Number Two (Bush & Lewis-Kulin, 2017; Levering et al., 2016).

Google benefits include free gourmet food, laundry services, improved parental leave policies, and free rides to work (Lashinsky, 2020). Google's adhocracy culture includes frequent town halls, support for all workers, and unconscious-bias workshops fostering a safe and inclusive workplace. In addition, Google is generous; they have donated $50 million to thousands of nonprofits (Cameron & Quinn, 2011; Daft, 2016; Ferrell, Fraedrich, & Ferrell, 2019). A healthy organizational culture matters.

Leaders dedicated to DDM should promote the DDM philosophy: 1) achieving higher quality managerial decisions, 2) reiterating potential benefits of DDM decisions, and 3) instilling the company mantra, "DDM: Decisions with principles." Wegman's CEO Danny Wegman stated they look for people who genuinely care about others and are pleased to serve as needed; they can teach just about any skills they need. Wegmans boasts flexible schedules, abundant promotion chances, and a family-like clan culture (Cameron & Quinn, 2011; Daft, 2016). Birthday cakes, college scholarships, learning trips, and hot drinks for outside employees contribute to Wegman's positive culture. As stated, these benefits indicate an appreciation for employees' valued contributions (Levering et al., 2016).

AT&T has refocused its advertising. AT&T "is using the power of its brand to improve the portrayal of women and diverse communities" (AT&T, 2019, p. 16). Fiona Carter, the Chief Brand Officer, contends, "A lot of companies talk about corporate social responsibility. We look at it more like corporate social action. As one of the largest advertisers in the country, when [AT&T] makes a change, it has a significant impact" (p. 16). AT&T, Number Nine in the 2019 Fortune 500, is considerate of its employees (Colvin, 2019).

The Google, Wegmans, and AT&T's apparent positive organizational cultures are destined:

- To improve organizational performance

- To increase employee job satisfaction and

- To enhance organizational reputations

The researcher argues that Google, Wegmans, and AT&T's benefits and goal attainments have correlated positively using decision models, perhaps similar to DDM capabilities. Displays of employee appreciation require managerial planning. There is usually an array of organization operating goals: market share, inventory goals, financial goals, production, and sales, as discussed by Cyert and March (1992). Of current interest are financial goals. In their book, *Business Essentials*, Ebert and Griffin (2015) stressed the importance of goal setting. People-oriented managers' plan and budget for benefits such as scholarships, free gourmet food, bonuses, and free rides to work. To conclude, astute managers understand the budgeting process and leverage it to demonstrate an appreciation of their workforce. It appears that Google, Wegmans, and AT&T managers optimized their financial budgeting on behalf of their employees. (For early and later perspectives on operational goals and navigating that process see Cyert & March, 1992; Ebert & Griffin, 2015; and Perrow, 1961).

Bear in mind Perrow's (1961) historical perspective that operational goals in which actual goals emerge only when the public or official goal is factored into operational goals. This appears to be the case for Wegmans. Consideration of people and concern for time, financials, the organization, and moral and ethical implications are the essence of DDM.

Wegmans has made *Fortune*'s "Best 100" lists every year since 1998. The 2018 list rated Salesforce© Number One and Wegmans Number Two. Google's parent company Alphabet rated Number 22 in 2018. In *Fortune*'s 2019, Wegmans rated Number Three (Bush & Tkczyk, 2019). In *Fortune*'s 2019 "Best Workplaces for Diversity," Wegmans rated Number Four (Bush, & Lewis-Kulin, 2017; Marya, 2019). These companies have continued positive, sustainable business practices.

Analogously, Google, Wegmans, and AT&T have demonstrated near similar DDM outcomes are possible. DDM's decision philosophy creates the opportunity for such decisions, primarily because of its systematic nature, structure, objectivity, and subjectivity.

3 DDM and CCS Theoretical Perspectives

DDM, a theoretical prescriptive model, supports and builds upon the well-established tenet that managers should make rational decisions rather than only good-enough or satisficing ones. Optimal refers to achieving the best or most favorable outcome, given the situation, opportunity, and resources to make as perfect or effective [a decision] as possible (Bell, Raiffa, & Tversky, 1988; Simon, 1997). DDM consists of eight tenets:

- DDM is a prescriptive management-centered decision process. Senior management is responsible for introducing, training, implementing, maintaining, and evaluating managers' DDM effectiveness annually.

- DDM institutionalization as a management innovation. Leaders should instill the mantra "DDM: Decisions with principles."

- DDM producing a higher-quality decision, which means achieving an above-average to very beneficial outcome, given contextual constraints

- DDM five interdependent Domains are people, time, financials, the organization, and moral and ethical implications, all subject to both internal and external scrutiny

- DDM operational mediating variables evaluate, question, and research; the process mediating variables are proactive communication, proactive integration, proactive coordination, and proactive collaboration

- DDM systematic, structured, and repetitive processes

- DDM objective quantitative component, and

- DDM subjective qualitative component

Management-Centered

March and Simon (1958) in *Organizations* assert, "Most human decision-making, whether individual or organizational, is concerned with the discovery and selection of satisfactory alternatives; only in exceptional cases is it concerned with the discovery and selection of optimal alternatives" (p. 162). Concurring with this viewpoint, DDM argues for a more comprehensive and structured process.

DDM is a prescriptive management-centered decision-making process. Senior managers are responsible for introducing, training, implementing and maintaining DDM. Without this from-the-top emphasis, DDM benefits are in jeopardy. For today's managers challenged with the competition, sustainability, and the opioid crisis, DDM is an opportunity to improve one's decision acuity (Nachtwey, 2018; Fortune.com, 2018; Roger, 2019).

Chevron's financial disbursements demonstrated the likenesses of Domains of Decision Management (DDM) characteristics. Chevron's 2017 dividend disbursement, to this researcher, was an indicator of a repetitive, structured, objective, and institutionalized decision process. That annual per-share dividend payout increased for the 30th consecutive year. Chevron also strengthened its balance sheet – its year-end debt ratio was 20.7 percent, down from 24.1 percent at 2016 year-end (Chevron, 2018). Such financials were very beneficial to Chevron shareholders (Bell, Raiffa, & Tversky, 1988; Keeny, & Raiffa, 1976). A DDM higher-quality decision means an outcome between above-average and very beneficial (termed advantageous or valuable). Operationally, higher-quality means outcomes of between above-average and very beneficial.

Drucker on Effective Decisions

Peter Drucker (1966), the management sage, noted that "Effective executives...make effective decisions using a systematic process with clearly defined elements and by following a sequence of steps" (p. 113). Drucker's paraphrased essential decision steps:

- Decide if the decision situation, in today's vernacular, programmed or non-programmed, stated differently, is it a routine reoccurring situation or a new and novel one, which occurs infrequently

- State the details, specifications, and objectives of the expected decision outcome

- Begin with "what is right rather than what is acceptable" (p. 134)

- Appoint a responsible person to manage and monitor decision implementation, and

- Schedule periodic feedback sessions to assess the need for implementation tweaking (1966)

Similarly, DDM is a systematic process having clearly defined elements, people, time, financials, the organization, and moral and ethical implications, following a distinct sequence of operational steps.[*]

A Repetitive Process

A repetitive process serves researchers and practitioners well. Researchers at the University of Pittsburgh revealed establishing and main-

---

[*]   Decision making essentials summarized from pp. 113, 122-123, 134 of *The Effective Executive* by Peter F. Drucker. Copyright (©) 1966, 1967 by Peter F. Drucker. Copyright renewed 1994, 1995 by Peter F. Drucker. Used by permission of HarperCollins Publishers.

taining a morning exercise regimen has lasting benefits throughout the workday, so much so, that it improves one's decision-making abilities (Bahler, 2019). Brain imaging indicated the brain's prefrontal cortex controls two essential functions: decision-making and anxiety, which may adversely affect some people since these two functions may be in opposition, thus making decisions difficult. Sarah Wilson (2018), in her recent book, *First, We Make the Beast Beautiful,* has found a way to lessen anxiety by consistently taking a morning run regardless of the weather; this counteracts harmful prefrontal cortex emanations. Her repetitive exercise routine mimics other repetitive routines by well-known thinkers: author Seth Godin's repetitive breakfast meal; Facebook's Mark Zuckerberg's repetitive gray T-shirt, similar to the late Steve Jobs; and Vogue® editor Anna Wintour waking each morning to a 5:45 a.m. repetitive tennis match (Bahler, 2019). These accomplished individuals benefited from maximizing a repetitive process. Likewise, DDM's core tenet is a repetitive process of detailed evaluating, questioning, and researching.

Prescriptive and Structured

DDM is *prescriptive* and *structured.* Steps to improve one's decision skills may entail being open to new ideas, assessing a process step-by-step, and receiving more education. Taking positive steps like these could make a quantum leap in one's decision skills (Bell, Raiffa, & Tversky, 1988; Simon, 1997). Figure 1 distinguishes among the *rational, descriptive,* and *prescriptive* decision approaches. Equally important, DDM is a *structured* process. It is prearranged and ordered ensuring managers, staffers, and employees understand their DDM duties and responsibilities – an essential role. This contributes to DDM effectiveness.

General Motors (GM)* recently demonstrated that higher-quality decisions utilize quantitative and qualitative components. When GM announced the closure of several manufacturing facilities and cutting nearly 14,800 employment positions, this was a sustainable business decision, due to weak sedan sales. "To help GM sustain profits through an expected downturn in the US car market and keep investing in burgeoning technologies," stated the GM CEO (Colias,

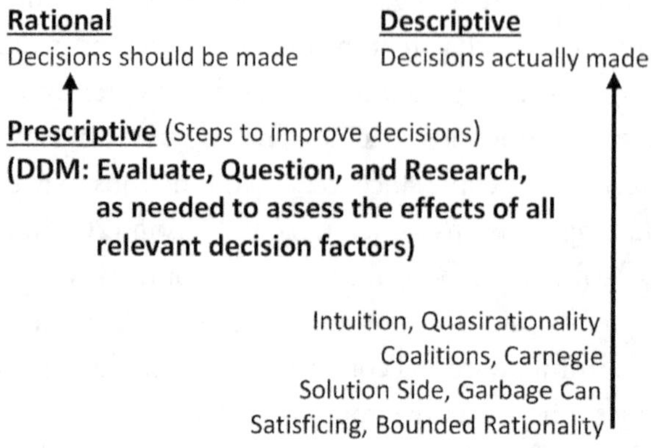

Rational   **Descriptive**
Decisions should be made   Decisions actually made

↑   ↑

Prescriptive (Steps to improve decisions)
**(DDM: Evaluate, Question, and Research,
        as needed to assess the effects of all
        relevant decision factors)**

Intuition, Quasirationality
Coalitions, Carnegie
Solution Side, Garbage Can
Satisficing, Bounded Rationality

Figure 1. Relationships among rational, descriptive, and prescriptive decision approaches. Rational and prescriptive approaches are usually more structured and manageable than descriptive approaches. Groundings: (Cohen, March, & Olsen, 1972; Cyert & March, 1963; Hammond, 2010; March & Simon, 1958; Pfeffer, 1981; Simon, 1997).

2018, p. A1). To remain competitive, CEO Mary Barra continued, "We think it's appropriate to get in front of it while the business and the economy are strong" (p. A1). From a quantitative perspective, the company expects to save $4.3 billion by the end of 2020. Quantitative and qualitative information provided relevant and timely decision data. Analogous to DDM philosophy, this GM decision is demonstrating nearly similar outcomes as a DDM examination.

Where DDM Theory Fits, Internal and External Scrutiny

DDM is prescriptive. Operationally, DDM systematically guides management, staff, and employees in evaluating, questioning, and researching via the processes of proactive communication, integration, coordination, and collaboration. Further, DDM contributes as an institutionalized management innovation, as discussed by Daft (2016) and, in part, by March and Simon (1958). Company mantra, "DDM: Decisions with principles."

Table 2

Integrating Domains of Decision Management (DDM)© and a Rational Model

---

Rational and Prescriptive Unity:

- **Identifies** and defines the problem, issue, or opportunity.
- **Evaluates** the alternatives that include integrating the DDM variables into the evaluating, questioning, and researching process; the DDM process means determining the effects all alternatives have on the five Domains – people, time, financials, the organization, and moral and ethical implications.
- **Implements** selected alternative and re-evaluates at periodic intervals

The five Domains are evaluated internally and externally maximizing DDM's repetitive evaluating, questioning, and researching tenets. See the DDM instructions and worksheets in Appendix B.

See Table 2. Managers utilizing any rational model augmented with the DDM model would evaluate, question, and research the pending decision's impact on the five Domains. This means evaluating, questioning, and researching the potential decision's internal and external impact on each Domain. Internal refers to potential decision impacts within the organization, for example, impacts on employees, management, and staff. Differently, external refers to potential decision impacts outside the organization, such as impacts on customers, suppliers, and applicable stakeholders. DDM can play a significant supportive role in any rational decision-making process. Arguably, subjecting any problem, issue, or opportunity to a thorough DDM evaluation can result in a very beneficial decision, thus contributing to improved organizational performance.

Mediating Variables, Double-loop, and Critical Thinking

DDM© is structured with dynamic interactions of evaluative uniformity. A *very beneficial* decision is the *dependent* variable, while the five Domains are *independently* acting ones. According to Yin (2018), variables, in their traditional qualitative sense, and variables, in their case study sense, remain controversial (p. xxiii). Even so, intervening between the independent and dependent variables are the staffing actions of *evaluating, questioning,* and *researching* potential decision impacts; these are operational *mediating* variables. These mediating variables are akin to Argyris's double-loop learning and questioning in which repetitive questioning examines the problem, issue, or opportunity (1991).

In total, seven mediating variables are positioned purposefully between the independent variables and the dependent variable in an influencing mode. These mediating variables influence the independent and dependent variables, but only for a limited time (Creswell, 2014; Leedy & Ormrod, 2019). The variables act in *operational* and *process* roles. However, if management, staff, or employees evaluate, question, or research at less than maximum collective work effort, expect decision quality to be diminished. See Figure 2, the DDM Model, to appreciate the mediating variables.

Last, integral to the DDM process is critical thinking, *asking the right questions,* which ensures a logical and objective examination. Browne and Keeley (2015) define *critical thinking* as having, "An awareness of a set of interrelated critical questions, plus the ability and willingness to ask and answer them at appropriate times"(p. 5). "Plus the ability and willingness," from above, may be the human "X" factor in the DDM Model. If managers are not fully committed to DDM, the absence of *willingness* could be the difference between success and failure. Bear in mind; there is no guarantee that all decisions emanating from DDM evaluation will be to everyone's liking; some outcomes may be very beneficial, and some may resemble the GM decision to release 14,000 workers. The only solace would be the decision resulted from a thorough DDM examination. See Appendix C for additional probing questions supporting evaluation and questioning.

When decision practitioners replace short-term thinking with DDM focused thought of the organization's stakeholders, employees, and customers' balanced, best interest, it may result in a prudent finding. The finding that, "High morale leads to high productivity; good leadership (i.e., 'democratic' leadership, good human relations, and consideration) leads to high morale, and thus to high productivity." These conclusions, still relevant today, are resident in Miles' human resources model (Miles, 1965, pp. 148-155).

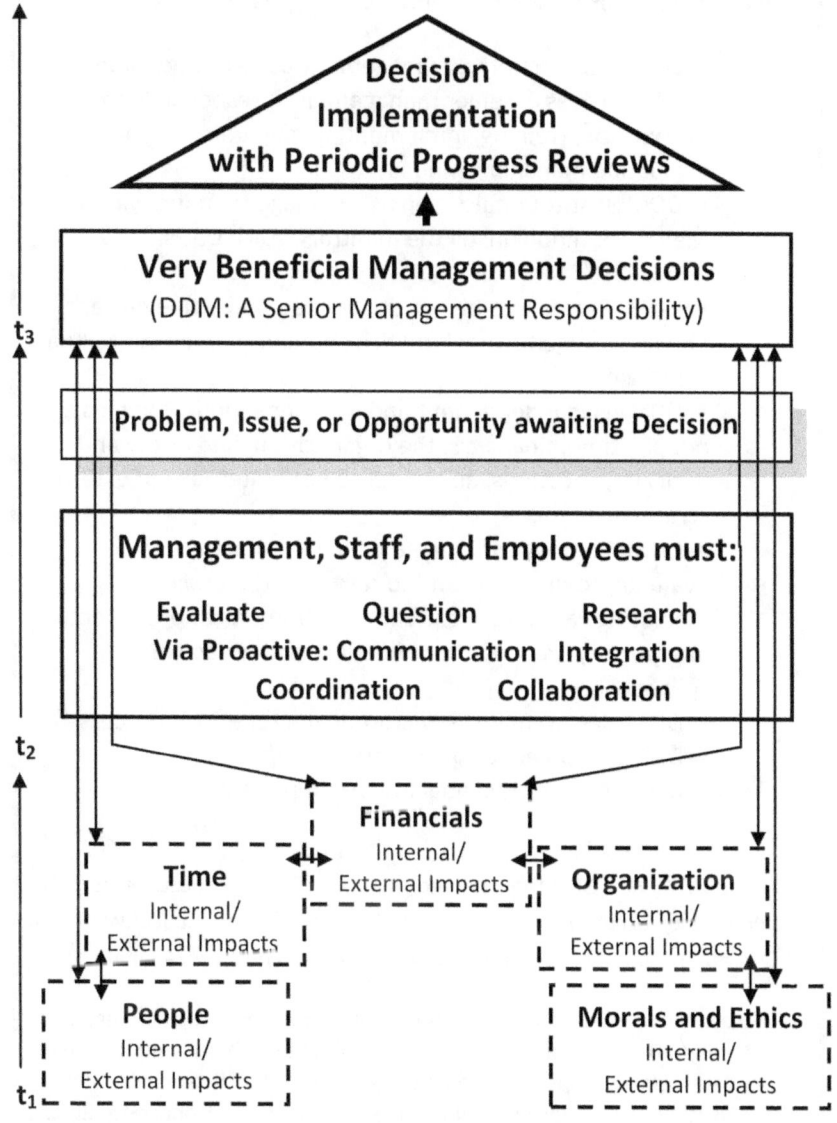

Figure 2.
Domains of Decision Management (DDM) Model

Figure 2. **Domains of Decision Management (DDM) Model.** To achieve higher-quality decisions, managers should systematically examine five Domains before making final decisions. DDM consists of eight tenets:

- DDM: A prescriptive management-centered decision-making process. Senior management is responsible for introducing, training, implementing, maintaining, and evaluating managers annually
- DDM: Institutionalization as a management innovation. Managers should instill the mantra, "DDM: Decisions with principles."
- DDM: Produces a higher-quality decision, achieving an above-average to very beneficial outcome, given contextual constraints
- DDM: Five independent and interdependent Domains are people, time, financials, the organization, and moral and ethical implications, all subject to both internal and external scrutiny
- DDM: The *operational* mediating variables are to evaluate, to question, and to research; the *process* mediating variables are proactive communication, proactive integration, proactive coordination, and proactive collaboration
- DDM: A systematic, structured, and repetitive process
- DDM: An objective quantitative component, and
- DDM: A subjective qualitative component

Use one DDM Worksheet per decision option. *Condition descriptors* (CD), *probability of occurrence* (PO), *expected value* (EV), and *collective totals* (CT) compare multiple decision options. A *question* begins examination.

Two-way arrows indicate multidirectional evaluating, questioning, and researching. Dashed Domain boundaries facilitate symbiotic and resource-dependent relationships. Groundings: (Argyris, 1991; Browne & Keeley, 2015; Drucker, 1966; Ferrell, Fraedrich, & Ferrell, 2019; Honekopp, 2003; Leedy & Ormrod, 2019; March & Simon, 1958; Mosier, 1989; Stogdill & Coons, 1957).

Collective Case Study (CCS) Theoretical Prospective

This theoretical perspective builds upon established collective case study (CCS) doctrine that utilizes Boolean logic, modified for CCS purposes. Boolean logic's dichotomous reasoning component was most practical in evaluating the *presence* (1) or *absence* (0) of the Literature Review decision factors.

Rather than a traditional case study Truth Table, an *induction* strategy was more substantive. An induction strategy collects pertinent evidence that permits the researcher to infer conclusions. Induction was instrumental in the finding that Wells Fargo and VW were victims of decision factor similarities, which made the companies *reasonably comparable* (Carucci, 2016; Glazer, 2016a; and Bach, 2015; Mahler, 2015, respectively; Schwandt, 2015).

Case study is a quest for comparative evidence. *Evidence* refers to information and facts of the case useful in forming a conclusion (Jonsen & Toulmin, 1998; Schwandt, 2015).

Yin (2018) states that case study is preferred when: 1) "The researcher seeks knowledge regarding *how* or *why*, 2) when the researcher uses multiple sources of evidence, and 3) when the researcher has no control, in this study, of the decision environments" (as cited in Schwandt, 2015, p. 27). Stake (1995) posits, "The foremost concern of case study research is to generate knowledge of the particular. Stake favors case studies that aim to discern and pursue an understanding of issues intrinsic to the case itself" (as cited in Schwandt, 2015, p. 27).

Intrinsic to the Wells Fargo and VW collective case study were problematic managerial decisions and outcomes.

Yin's (2018) asserted to utilize a case study to ascertain both how and why; Leedy and Ormrod (2019) counter that view and state a "Quantitative study determines how and why, and cause-and-effect" (p. 230). Also, Yin (2018) advised, "Variables, in their traditional qualitative sense, and variables in their case study sense, remain controversial" (p. xxiii). These dichotomous views caused the researcher to also employ a three-person expert panel, each familiar with organizational decision processes. The CCS evidence from the Literature

Review linked to conclusions via *induction*, a strategy of collecting a plethora of relevant evidence, and then inferring conclusions (Schwandt, 2015). See Figure 3. Subsequently, a quantitative computation determined the factor ordering from the most significant influencing factor (1st place) to the least influencing factor (5th place).

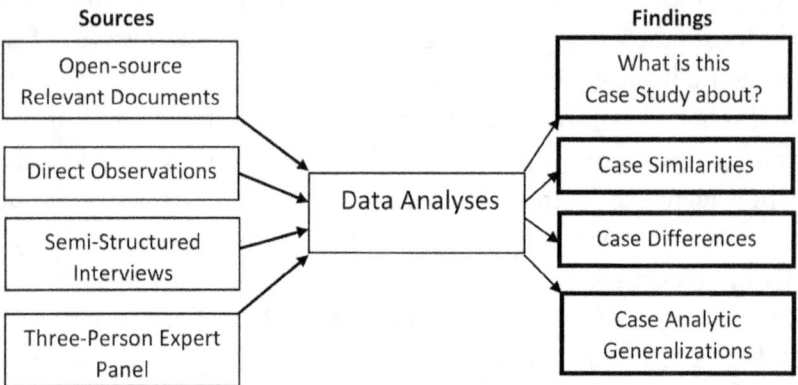

Sources   Findings

| Open-source Relevant Documents |
| Direct Observations |
| Data Analyses |
| Semi-Structured Interviews |
| Three-Person Expert Panel |

| What is this Case Study about? |
| Case Similarities |
| Case Differences |
| Case Analytic Generalizations |

Figure 3. **Collective Case Study (CCS) Theoretical Perspective. To realize CCS findings required extensive documents, time, and perseverance. Boolean algebra modified, pertinent Wells Fargo and Volkswagen documents, direct observations, semi-structured interviews, and a three-person expert panel, via *induction* allowed the case study findings to emerge. Data triangulation (the data sources) and theory triangulation (different perspectives of the same data set) played significant roles in the emergence of the findings. Groundings: (Bernard & Ryan, 2010; Jonsen & Toulmin, 1998; Leedy & Ormrod, 2019; Ragin, 2014; Ragin & Amoroso, 2011; Rhioux & Lobe, 2009; Rhioux & Ragin, 2009; Schwandt, 2015; Stake, 1995; Yin, 2018).**

QCA functions as follows:

QCA uses a small number of cases, in this study, Wells Fargo and VW, both comparable. Each case is viewed as a combination of influencing factors linked to the decision outcomes. Next, the researcher examines each case and determines whether influencing factors and outcomes are either "present or absent," thus producing a matrix specifying the configurations of causes that produced the outcome.[1]

1. Adapted from discussion of qualitative comparative analysis and the researcher's role (Bernard & Ryan, 2010 (For a very brief introduction to the method); Ragin & Amoroso, 2011 (For a slightly longer but accessible introduction to the method by its originator); Rhioux & Lobe, 2009 discuss QCA in B. Byrne & C. C. Ragin, Eds., (2009). *Handbook of Cross-Case Methods*. London, England: Sage; and Rhioux & Ragin, 2009, (as cited in Schwandt, 2015, p. 255).

4 Worldview: Philosophical Truth and Knowledge Claims

A worldview refers to "a basic set of beliefs that guide action" (Guba, 1990, p. 17). An evaluation of multiple worldviews – positivism, constructionism, and pragmatism – were appropriate for determining suitability for the DDM and collective case study (CCS) research (Creswell, 2014; Sekaran & Bougie, 2016).

Worldview decisions result in particular research methods and procedures. Hofweber (2013) defines ontology as the philosophical study and examination of the nature of existence, being, or reality; to study and contemplate problems concerning whether a particular thing exists. Ontology investigates existence, such as is it possible to know the truth?

Understanding ontology's purpose, is it possible to know the truth regarding the subject Wells Fargo and VW decision environments? It may be possible. Is it possible to know the total truth regarding Wells Fargo and VW decisions concerning cross-sells and clean-diesel, respectively? Total truth, probably not. However, it may be possible to draw reasonable conclusions from collecting data, conducting interviews, and making observations describing company cultures, decision environments, and other pertinent decision factors. Brief discussions follow.

Positivism

Positivism is the belief that there exists an objective truth. It also holds that the world operates on a series of cause-and-effect laws. These actions and reactions are discerned through a scientific process – a quantitative study. In this worldview, phenomenon such as emotions, thoughts, and feelings are impossible to investigate. Descriptive characteristics of quantitative inquiry include theory testing, rigor, replicability, and objective measures. Positivists consider research to occur via direct observation and objective measure. The DDM researcher utilized its theory testing and objective measure qualities (Sekaran & Bougie, 2016).

Constructionism

The constructionism worldview relies on one's subjective experiences. This perspective acknowledges that individuals seek understanding of a complex world, and individuals generate subjective meanings of their experiences – meanings toward particular objects and things. Respondent views are paramount. Research questions may be open-ended, allowing the respondent to respond freely and thoroughly in his or her life setting. This worldview prides itself on respondent interactions and textual descriptions. The works of Berger and Luckmann's *The Social Construction of Reality* (1967), and Lincoln and Guba's (1985) *Naturalistic Inquiry* ground this worldview. Respondent-rich dialogue together with peer debriefing reinforced research rigor and validity of the DDM findings (Creswell, 2013/ 2014; Leedy & Ormrod, 2019).

Pragmatism

The pragmatism worldview has a more expansive perspective. Pragmatists are open-minded and do not limit their research thinking. They believe the researcher should seek objective truth and subjective meanings for understanding. In other words, researchers should utilize a mixed-methods approach producing combined, integrated data, dual analysis, and comprehensive findings. Pragmatists view mixed-method findings as tentative. Because the DDM was a theoretical model, the broadest array of research tools seemed appropriate. However, true mixed-methods procedures would have prolonged the research beyond its completion date. While an exact mixed-method study was not employed, its spirit of gathering data from multiple sources was utilized. Perhaps future researchers will build upon this theoretical base with a mixed-methods study (Leedy & Ormrod, 2019; Sekaran & Bougie, 2016).

A collective case study with qualitative and quantitative components proved sufficient in gaining a deeper understanding of the Wells Fargo and VW decisions and DDM capabilities. These findings should assist managers challenged to make very beneficial decisions contributing to more ethical business behaviors and sustainable business practices.

5 Operational Definitions, Assumptions, and Scope

Operational definitions define characteristics or variables in terms of how they may be observed or measured in the study, or the reduction of abstract concepts to render them measurable in a tangible way (Leedy & Ormrod, 2019; Sekaran & Bougie, 2016). There were ten operational definitions.

- *Higher-quality* equates to an above-average to very beneficial management decision; the DDM's dependent variable. Very beneficial refers to decisions exhibiting advantageous and valuable qualities.

- *People, time, financials, the organization, and morals and ethics,* are independent variables. These five Domains of Decision Management are specified spheres of activity and knowledge. The Domains are interdependent because of the symbiotic and resource-dependent relationships existing among them. In brief, any less than maximum collective work effort of any one Domain may cause irreparable harm to the remaining interdependent Domains, and can threaten the organization's survivability (Creswell, 2014).

- *Evaluate, question, research, proactive integration, proactive communication, proactive coordination, and proactive collabo-*

ration are mediating variables. These variables are positioned between the dependent and independent variables in an influencing role. The first three variables are operative; the remaining four variables are process-oriented. In brief, any less than maximum collective work effort of any one Domain may cause irreparable harm to the remaining interdependent Domains, and can threaten the organization's survivability (Creswell, 2014).

- *Knowledgeable respondent.* An original definition. An individual with experience making managerial decisions or one who has observed ethical dilemmas, managerial decisions, and their consequences. Typically, these respondents discuss rich professional experiences during interviews.

- *Management innovation.* This is an emerging field of study that has a relatively small literature library. It is unique in that it involves the implementation of new management policies, practices, procedures, or organizational structures that influence and direct other types of innovation. The everyday purposes of management innovation allow for achieving organizational goals and competitive advantage (Daft, 2016; Nieves, 2016; Smith & Flanagan, 2006; Volberda, Van Den Bosch, & Hein, 2013).

- *Financial egoism.* An original definition. Individual, group, or organizational financial gain without regard for others who may be monetarily, physically, emotionally, or socially disadvantaged in some way. When this condition exists, it probably speaks to the root motivations of those who benefit.

- *Ethical dissonance.* This concept describes a sense of discomfort or distress that occurs when a person's ethical behavior does not correspond to his or her espoused ethical beliefs. In the Wells Fargo case, employee discomfort led many to leave the company searching for a more compatible organizational culture (Burchard, 2011; Fastinger, 1957).

- *Inherited decisions.* An original definition. Describes how individuals or groups may replicate or make decisions very similar to a previous individual or group. Typically, only minimal effort is exerted to evaluate other courses of action.

- *Golden Rule-type decisions* (GRTD). GRTD refers to a particular type of organizational decision philosophy. In other words, how senior management should consider and treat employees, customers, and applicable stakeholders. It is a belief that managerial decision-making should reflect the biblical *Golden Rule* that compels individuals to treat others the way they would like to be treated. To do so exhibits an excellent management stakeholder orientation. The Literature Review expounds on GRTD's meaning and its theological grounding (Kant, 1788; Mathews & Smith, 2015).

- *Respondent Experience Factor* (REF). Perceiving the DDM total sample of 33 as small, *representativeness bias* (Jones & George, 2014), ignores respondents' quality work experiences. This researcher understands their test item responses, qualitative and quantitative, resulted from $263.5 + 31 + 252 = 546.5$ years of practical decision-making experiences and employees observing the consequences of managerial decisions (see the 546.5 development details in **Research Methods**). This researcher interprets 546.5 years of decision-making together with observing the consequences of managerial decisions as quite significant. To capture this significance, the researcher developed this process to recognize quantitatively the small sample's years of valid work experience. Consider the term *Respondent Experience Factor* (REF), which adds significant weight to the representation of small qualitative and quantitative samples.

DDM Assumptions

Domains of Decision Management's (DDM) practical benefits rest on senior management's commitment to improving managerial decision quality. These assumptions act as the bedrock and self-evident truths underlying this prescriptive decision-making model, and they establish the DDM's organizational structure (Leedy & Ormrod, 2019). The assumptions are commensurate with the *initiating structure* construct from Ohio State University's behavioral management studies (Stogdill & Coons, 1957). Equally important, DDM's success is dependent on senior managers introducing, training, implementing, and maintaining the complete process, including accepting the axiom that knowledge equates to increased decision power. DDM requires managers who are functionally well trained and cognizant of organizational goals and priorities. The DDM assumptions:

- Require an organization of ethically minded managers (Ferrell, Fraedrich, & Ferrell, 2019). Leadership is paramount. Collins' (2001) Level 5 leadership qualities are not mandatory, but have demonstrated company success: personal humility, professional will, company first, self-effacing, compelling modesty, and understated. Kouzes and Posner's (2003) leader qualities have also demonstrated success: honesty, forward-looking, inspiring, competent, fair-minded, supportive, broad-minded, courageous, and caring, to name a few. Heid (2019) cited a Harvard University study finding that CEOs' noncognitive abilities are more important than their IQ score: noncognitive qualities include cooperation, self-control, social competence, and having a growth mindset. Self-control is also a noncognitive quality in emotional intelligence (EI). Additional EI qualities: empathy; sensitivity; being aware of one's own feelings and emotions, and understanding the feelings and emotions of others; being persistent regardless of obstacles; and having the ability to self motivate and to motivate others (Mayer & Salovey, 1997; Salovey & Mayer, 1990, [as cited in Ciccarelli & White, 2015]). Last, emulate the growth-minded leadership qualities of the late Jack Welch, former CEO and Board Chairman of General Electric (GE). His forward-looking strategies included: accepting change by all; listening for employees' good ideas; and challenging managers to position their products or services to be number one or number two in their respective markets; if not achieved "they would be shut down or sold off" (Slater, 2003, pp. 3-7).

- Establish the DDM as a management-centered process. Senior management is responsible for introducing, training, implementing, maintaining, and establishing DDM as a management innovation (March & Simon, 1958; Nieves, 2016; Steele, 2018).

- Require a *learning organization* where: people continually expand their capacity to create the results they desire, people develop new and unrestrained patterns of thinking, people make known their aspirations, and people continually engage in group learning (Senge, 1990).

- Establish the DDM as an evaluative component in performance appraisals. Evaluate managers and supervisors on their degree of DDM effectiveness during periodic performance appraisals (Dessler, 2018; Nor, Hollenbeck, Gerhart, & Wright, 2019).

- Require the DDM decision-making process to evaluate, question, and research via the processes of proactive communication, integration, coordination, and collaboration delegated to responsible managers within the organization.

- Establish a three-person Probability Decision Committee (PDC) to consider and determine the Probability of Occurrences (PO), as a functional element of the DDM Worksheet. See Appendix B. Vice President Level at a minimum is recommended. These individuals must be well versed in organizational operations, risk management, and company priorities.

- Maximize the usefulness of decision information by increasing its quality (i.e., accurate and reliable), timeliness (i.e., current and up-to-date), completeness (i.e., all that is necessary), and relevance (i.e., related to the matter at hand) (Jones & George, 2014).

Another example of personnel consideration and its consequences in the corporate world, in addition to Google ®, Wegmans ®, and AT&T ®, is the Professional Golfers Association (PGA). Considering the balanced interests of many regarding the 2020 coronavirus (COVID-19) pandemic, Jay Monahan, PGA Tour Commissioner, decided correctly announcing the cancellation of the prestigious Players Championship, and three additional tournaments. The three others were essentially warm-up play before the legendary Masters Tournament. To this researcher, amidst a dizzying list of cancellations and suspensions – the NBA, NHL, MLB, NCAA March Madness, among others (Calfas, 2020) - Monahan's decision environment was a complex of decision factors. Evaluating all, he made ethically appropriate decisions (Gleeson, 2020; Lynch, 2020).

This decision was not a solo decision. Monahan's decision emanated from a structured process of quality, timely, complete, and relevant information from diverse sources: International health authorities, federal government health agencies, state health agencies, affected tournament cities, and tournament sponsors (Lynch, 2020). The PGA's gathering of diverse information sources to clarify its decision environment mirrors DDM's Assumption to maximize the usefulness of decision information by increasing its quality (i.e., accurate and reliable), timeliness (i.e., current and up-to-date), completeness (i.e., all that is necessary), and relevance (i.e., related to the matter at hand) (Jones & George, 2014) (QTCR).

This researcher argues that PGA managers and staff evaluated, questioned, and researched the potential effects of their pending decisions on internal and external people, time, financials, the organization, and the moral and ethical perceptions of PGA partners and sponsors regarding indecision as opposed to making decisions to cancel and delay events. These PGA managers and staff actions resulted in group learning, and a steep learning curve - a learning organization quality (Senge, 1990). Having the latest information and consensus of thought from affected organizations and individuals, Commissioner Monahan addressed the media, demonstrating his competence to make judicious tough decisions (For additional details see Calfas, 2020; Glesson, 2020; and Lynch, 2020).

Scope of the Research

The Research Objectives define the scope of the DDM study and the Collective Case Study (CCS): 1) to describe what is this case study about, 2) to understand likely factors influencing specific Wells Fargo and Volkswagen executive decisions, and 3) to test a prescriptive theory that "managers may achieve above-average to very beneficial decisions by systematically evaluating five interdependent management Domains – people, time, financials, the organization, and moral and ethical implications." DDM's decision philosophy creates the opportunity for higher-quality decisions because of its convergence of structure, management oversight, and institutionalization as a management innovation; CCS was a quest for Wells Fargo and VW case evidence and decision enlightenment.

The Quest Continues

In the Preface, the researcher associated the Domains of Decision Management study with his early leadership experiences regarding consideration and people. Today's managers should be making decisions about taking care of people as well as the organization's bottom line. Discussion references to Chevron Corporation's financial performance; Jack Welch's (GE) innovative leadership; Google, Wegmans, and AT&T's consideration of employees; and Jay Monahan's prudent leadership of the PGA Tour, all support the contention that higher-quality decisions are possible, given the resolve of the decision maker.

Further, the researcher has argued when decision-makers fail to evaluate, question, and research decision consequences, decision implementation may become problematic. Such was arguably the case for Wells Fargo and Volkswagen. Questions remain as to what decision factors were most influential for both companies.

The quest for evidence and understanding continues. The Literature Review delves into organization theory and culture, social science influences, decision approaches, ethical counterviews, and innovative organization training options in an attempt to identify the factors causing these storied companies to tumble from being well respected to being reprehensible.

6 Literature Review: DDM Literature and CCS Evidence

The impetus for developing the DDM Model was improving the decision-making skills of managers; thus, *the unit of analysis*. The literature review examined a wide variety of likely independent variables, decision-making approaches, social-science concepts, and organization theories believed to be relevant to the Wells Fargo and VW cases. See Table 3. In addition, pertinent historical counterviews are discussed. They are deemed counter in the sense that mature adults may not believe such ethically indifferent motivations possible. Any thorough examination of likely decision factors must address a variety of possibilities, including intentional unethical decisions and financial egoism.

Literature searches in leadership, management, business, and education for a similar Domains of Decision Management discussion, theory, or model incorporating people, time, financials, the organization, and morals and ethics as independent variables, and the mediating variables of evaluating, questioning, researching, proactive communication, integration, coordination, and collaboration were fruitless. For that reason, these research findings should be a valuable tool in any manager's decision toolkit.

The Literature Review is composed of many poignant discussions. Following, now, are brief discussions of Enactment theory (Weick, 1969), Schein (2017) on organization culture, the changing nature of decision environments, Simon (1997) on bounded rationality, and Literature Review sources.

Enactment and Social Construction of Reality

The organization theory *symbolic perspective* (i.e., the 1980s) is rooted in *subjectivity* and *interpretation*. In brief, "*social facts* are as real as *objective facts*" (Hatch & Cunliffe, 2013, p. 33). Social facts, created via social interactions and other factors, are fundamental elements of the *constructionism* worldview, psychology's *social learning theory*, and the *sociology of knowledge* (Berger & Luckmann, 1967; Rohmann, 1999).

According to *enactment theory*, the environment managers respond to is the one they enact or create out of their perceptions (Weick, 1969); perceptions that may or may not be business sustainable, depending on their previous workplace and decision experiences, and whether their task and general environments are: *stable* or *unstable* (i.e., steady and constant or dynamic and changing), and *simple* or *complex* (i.e., heterogeneity or the number and variation of external vendors and other entities)(Daft, 2016). Such realities are difficult to negotiate.

An example *reality* was the one created by Bernard Madoff Investment Securities with his high-return investing strategies. New investors did receive such returns. Their word-of-mouth recommendations to friends expanded the Madoff myth. The social construction of reality further enlarged Madoff's reality because of its people interactions. Occurring simultaneously, long-time Madoff investors watched their returns become smaller and smaller. Some investors received no returns. At this point, several investors spoke to federal authorities (Maglich, 2013; Smith, 2009).

Madoff's business environment appeared to range from stable for new investors, to unstable and complex, for long-time investors. It was also complex when Madoff was dealing with federal regulators. Additionally, sometimes unstable and complex environments appear to have lives of their own, further complicating decision making, which was probably the case in Madoff's waning years.

To conclude, the WF and VW decision environments were similar in many ways to Madoff's complex and uncertain environments. WF and VW leadership appeared willing to set aside ethical rightness and customer considerations for, apparently, financial gain and improved market share (Ewing, 2019). There was no evidence of a devil's advocate or dialectical debate for either company.

WF: Present   VW: Present

Organization Culture Matters

Increased organizational performance, in part, depends on supportive ethical and considerate leadership, an informed and enthusiastic workforce, performance rewards, accumulated shared learning, positive individual growth, building on employee strengths, having an adaptive capability, and employees adhering to company's values. Collectively, these invaluable elements constitute a positive organizational culture that is essential to making very beneficial decisions (Edmondson, 2012; Nelson & Cooper, 2007; Schein, 2017). The culture also influences work practices and their style of operating (Gamble, Peteraf, & Thompson, 2017).

To conclude, no evidence was found citing positive cultural elements for either Wells Fargo or VW. However, evidence was found describing both cultures in several derogatory ways.

WF: Absent   VW: Absent

Decision Environment

Ironically, these same elements of culture or the lack thereof, are instrumental in defining an organization's decision environment. Decision environments, in this context, are exclusive to each company and may vary daily exerting multiple decision influences.

To conclude, as discussed, evidence has shown WF and VW contended with similar competitive, complex, and uncertain decision environments. Taken collectively, such variations in the decision environments placed added stress on decision makers.

WF: Present   VW: Present

Simon's Bounded Rationality

Simon's (1997) research regarding "how managers actually make decisions" was a landmark. Not only did Simon provide insight about how managers actually make decisions, he also found that decision-makers, to some degree, possess a limited cognitive capacity to process information, which he termed *bounded rationality*. These findings resulted in Herbert A. Simon receiving the 1978 Nobel prize in economics from the Royal Academy of Sciences. Even Perrow (2014), in his work *Complex Organizations*, asserted, "Organizations would function better if human rationality were less bounded. . . .If our rationality were full, no one could put anything over on us or shape our premises" (p. 123). To counter bounded rationality, DDM argues for more complete and actionable decision information adding clarity to any pending problem, issue, or opportunity.

WF: Present   VW: Present

Literature Review Sources

Scrutinized were periodicals, national newspapers for current information, and seminal works: Berger and Luckmann (1967), Blanchard and Johnson (1982), Cyert and March (1963), Drucker (1966/2001), Festinger (1957), Kant (1788), Kohlberg (1969), Kouzes and Posner (2003), Janis (1982), Lincoln and Guba (1985), March and Simon (1958), Perrow (2014), Pfeffer and Salancik (2003), Peters and Waterman (1982), Porter (1985), Schein (2017), Senge (1990), Stogdill and Coons (1957), Urban (2003), Weick (1969), among others. The DDM and CCS studies examined a wide range of sources, resulting in many cogent insights. Similar to a mixed-methods approach that embraces relevant information from diverse sources, so also did these studies. The DDM and CCS sources were priceless. The triangulation of data sources was crucial.

Unbiased Concluding Observations

Each Table 3 discussion ends with an unbiased concluding observation regarding the likelihood that that variable influenced the Wells Fargo or VW decisions. These were based on:

- The researcher's years of professional work experiences of considering and making workplace decisions and learning from decision consequences.

- Twenty-one years as an active duty US Army officer (LTC, Lieutenant Colonel), managing people, tasks, resources, decision making, and observing decision consequences.

- Observing pitfalls that often influence working group decisions.

- One year specialized aerospace industry training in Information Systems Management (ISM) with the Boeing Company. The Program Manager for the ISM program stated, "We recommend a variety of job assignments to expose the student to a wide range of management techniques and current processes" (Moffett, 1988, p.12). The curriculum included specialized rotating job assignments, project meetings, and quarterly lunches with senior management executives.

- Thirty-two years as a business owner, and manager of people, resources, and decisions, and

- Twenty-eight years lecturing at three different universities on physical science, leadership, management, business ethics, critical thinking, business research, and decision making.

To illustrate an unbiased concluding observation, here is one example. The Garbage-can conclusion states: "To conclude, typically, management decision information abounds in business strategy sessions; therefore, garbage-can decisions were ruled out as possible influences." See the extended Literature Review, Table 3.

Collective Case Study (CCS) Qualitative Comparative Analysis (QCA)

Early evidence found that Wells Fargo (Carucci, 2016; Egan, 2016; Glazer 2016a) and VW (Bach, 2015; Hakim, Kessler, & Ewing, 2015; Mahler, 2015) were victims of similar decision factors. Even so, this finding did not compromise the researcher's integrity. All biases and preconceived notions were suspended as in phenomenological studies, as discussed in Husserl (2000) and Moustakas (1994). The researcher allowed the three research approaches, collective case study, qualitative, and quantitative, to unfold within their prescribed methodologies. Following each discussion, a QCA dichotomous determination is made regarding that topic being a likely decision-influencing factor contributing to Wells Fargo and VW problematic decisions. Following each is, WF: Present VW: Present or WF: Absent VW: Absent.

Table 3

Literature Review: Likely Wells Fargo and Volkswagen Decision Factors and Discussions

(Decision environment: An original definition. Boehmer, (2001); Daft (2016); Jones and George (2014); Mason (1969); Soukhanov (1984); and Schweiger and Finger (1984)	**Decision environment,** in this study, refers to the complexity of social, cultural, ethical, and business forces and phenomena influencing the nature of individual or group decisions. For both Wells Fargo (WF) and Volkswagen (VW) their decision environments were influenced by multiple factors. Further, having a strong *devil's advocate* question the preferred option's assumptions, assertions, and potential outcomes may render that option unacceptable. Also, *dialectical inquiry*, even though it is more time consuming, is a more thorough decision process in which multiple options are debated before senior executives (Mason, 1969; Schweiger & Finger, 1984). To conclude, no documents were found indicating WF or VW utilized either devil's advocacy or dialectical inquiry. Both decision environments were likely influenced, to some degree, by several decision factors resulting in the WF and VW problematic outcomes. An examination of likely decision factors follows.
	WF: Present VW: Present

Botti and Cloney (2016); Kida, Moreno, and Smith (2010)

Paradox of choice refers to there being *many choices* or *too many choices*, from which to select. A paradox of choice may have complicated reasoning and decision making for WF and VW. Financial research found that executives (exec.) knowledgeable about financial issues required less time to make decisions, which suggests the paradox of choice phenomena may not apply in all cases. To conclude, this could imply that WF and VW made intentionally problematic decisions.

WF: Absent   VW: Absent

Dhami and Thomson (2012); Hammond (2010)

Quasirationality decisions combine intuition and a degree of reasoning. Hammond (2010) its originator, argues these in-between forms of cognition activity are referred to as quasirational, that is, as resembling rationality rather than being identical with it. He argued the greater part of our cognitive activity is quasirational; it is the normal or of cognition-human judgment that is, neither fully analytical nor fully intuitive but involves different amounts of each, depending on which attributes are present in our normal activities. Hammond also recognized that quasirationality fails to achieve logical perfection due to an absence of current knowledge. To conclude, quasirationality, or other decision models, likely failed due to insufficient future-market information or incorrect judgments, thus contributing to WF and VW problematic decisions.

WF: Present   VW: Present

Boehmer (2001); Cyert and March (1963); March and Simon (1958); Pfeffer (1981)

Carnegie Model refers to decisions made through alliances and coalitions of individuals that align themselves with the most politically or well-informed managers and persons present. Often, coalitions arise because of ill-defined organizational goals, inconsistent operative goals, and the inherent bounded rationality of the decision-makers. In such cases, alliances will form supporting universal points of interest, such as continuation of the WF sales strategy and the VW deception. To conclude, the WF and VW current business models were very good sources of income, why change? Apparently, no strong devil's advocate present. From the researcher's decision experiences, alliances and coalitions were significant influencing factors for WF and VW.

WF: Present   VW: Present

Cohen, March, and
Olsen (1972)

Garbage-can decision-makers begin the process in a fashion that counters any rational model. Garbage-can decisions begin from the *solution side* rather than from the *problem side*. Such decision making results from a random and chaotic process of attaching solutions to problems. At times, it creates more problems than it solves. Despite the chaos, some problems are still re-solved. Was garbage-can decision making a culprit in the WF and VW cases? Arguably, not, because these type decisions emerge from fragmented and often incomplete information, which probably was not the case for these two well-resourced corporations. To conclude, typically, management (mgt) decision information abounds in business strategy sessions; therefore, garbage-can decisions were ruled out as influencing WF and VW decisions.   WF: Absent   VW: Absent

Back (2016);
Carucci (2016);
Ciccarelli and White
(2015);
Clozel and Ackerman
(2019)
Cowley and Flitter
(2018);
Egan, (2016)
Flitter, Appelbaum, and
Enrich (2018);
Flitter, Cowley, and
Enrich (2019);
Glazer (2016a, b);
Glazer (2017a,b,c);
Glazer (2018);
Stewart (2018);
Tracy (2018);
Wells Fargo Bank
(2017)

Corporate governance failures. Carucci (2016) argued WF possessed an unethical culture. Strict sell targets: Family of five had 81 accounts (Glazer, 2017c). Unethical cross-selling was profitable and endorsed by top WF execs. The Board seemed to ignore its risk mgt and ethics responsibilities; the Federal Central Bank ordered WF to replace four Board members: reduced from 16 to 12. Assets held at $2 trillion. Fired: approx 5,300 employees (many blackballed), and about three dozen District Managers. The bank settled related state investigations for $575 million. Approx total settlement costs $2.240 billion. A senior WF exec argued to US regulators WF was fixing its issues, to no avail. March 2019, WF CEO testified before US House; he resigned March 29, 2019.

Bomey (2018);
Boston (2018);
Ewing (2017a, b);
Ewing (2018);
Ewing (2019);
Ewing and Mouawad
(2015);
Hakim, Kessler, &
Ewing (2015);
Mahler (2015);
McGee (2019a);
McGee and Storbeck
(2019);
Roberts (2017);
VAP (2018);
Gates et al. (2015);
Smith and Flanagan
(2006)

(Corporate governance failures, cont.)

Mercedes, VW, and Audi agreed to share clean-diesel (CD) tech. Mercedes introduced its CD in 2006; VW developed its CD ca. 2006. The CD, an illegal emissions computer switch, existent ca. 2008 to 2015. The VW Board was not informed prior to public notice. Dec. 2018, VAP argued VW's corrupt culture was reintroducing thousands of rejected vehicles back to market, however, researcher interviews with VW Sales Managers found a valid business model of repair and sale. Eight VW execs charged with CD crimes. Costs: $30 billion plus.

VW admitted to having a toxic culture and authoritarian leadership in pursuit of becoming the world leader, win-at-all-cost (Eddy, 2019; Ewing, 2019). To conclude, WF and VW were competing for market share. Both WF and VW were victimized by failed leadership and Boards that failed to protect from financial and reputational risk, thus contributing greatly to flawed WF and VW decision outcomes. Apparently, no devil's advocate was present.

WF: Present   VW: Present

(Inherited decisions: An original definition) Abdellah (2016); Burchard (2011); Daft (2016); Fastinger (1957); Janis (1982); Jones and George (2014); Pfeffer and Salancik (2003)

Social science possibilities: *ethical dissonance, group-think,* and *inherited decisions. Ethical dissonance* refers to a person's disturbed ethical feelings, heightened emotions, and attitudes resulting from the incongruity between his or her actual behavior and his or her espoused ethical values and preferred behaviors. Anecdotally, this was often the case for frustrated WF employees, which resulted in many employees leaving the company for less stress-filled employment. *Groupthink,* according to Janis and Daft, occurs when decision options are not fully investigated because of individual propensities to go along with the group to maintain harmony and good feelings. Also, decision-makers may reject decisions because of matters not related to the issue at hand. *Inherited decisions.* WF and VW decision-makers appear to have figuratively inherited past decision-making patterns because the status quo was profitable. Were there decision constraints? Pfeffer and Salancik (2003) discussed organizational constraints within similar business circumstances in which they argued, "Most constraints on organizational actions are the result of prior decision making or the resolution of various conflicts among competing interest groups" (p. 18). Or was it *prior-hypothesis* bias in which "decisions may be based on strong prior beliefs even though current evidence dispels such beliefs as untrue or false?" (Jones & George, 2014, p. 209). Either of the above may have been suspect. To conclude, groupthink, because of a strong desire to maintain group harmony, was likely a key factor in the WF and VW decisions. Apparently, no strong devil's advocate was present.

WF: Present   VW: Present

Peters and Waterman (1982)

In, *In Search of Excellence,* Peters and Waterman argued for managers to have a bias for action and a preference for doing something rather than becoming stuck or stymied in continual analyses. Such action and decision-making are supported if there exists sufficient information, time, and resources to evaluate, question, and research potential decision outcomes. Otherwise, an inappropriate decision is likely. To conclude, WF and VW execs likely displayed a penchant for action, and became mired in debate and frustration, resulting in problematic decisions.   WF: Absent   VW: Absent

Sitkin and Lind (2018)

Six Domains of Leadership (DoL), developed in the Duke University Leadership Academy, consist of *personal, relational, contextual, inspirational, supportive*, and *responsible*. These qualities appear to function more as prescriptive *leadership* qualities, rather than a purposeful prescriptive, repetitive, structured, and institutionalized managerial decision-making process. Further, these DoL steps are unlike the DDM tenets that have the focused purpose of elevating the quality of organizational managerial decisions from acceptable ones to *very beneficial* ones. To conclude, while the DoL accomplishes a leadership purpose, had WF and VW adhered to its *Responsibility* quality, their decision outcomes likely would not have been problematic.

WF: Absent   VW: Absent

Dessler (2001)

Dessler's Prescription. His listing describes actions intended to improve one's decision-making skills. The listing consists of *being creative, checking assumptions, exercising process analysis, increasing one's knowledge, de-biasing one's judgement, using one's intuition, recognizing that decisions are seldom final,* and *making sure the timing is right* (pp. 109-115). These prescriptive behaviors were individually focused with no *from-the-top* mandate, referring to a top management emphasis. To conclude, had WF and VW execs thought critically, exercised thorough process analysis, de-biased their judgements, and collaborated with their respective Boards, the quality of their decisions may have averted problematic decisions.

WF: Absent   VW: Absent

Dessler's Prescription for Decision Improvement (For Individuals)	
Be creative	Right timing matters
Check assumptions	Evaluate one's intuition
Exercise process analysis	Decisions are seldom final
Withhold one's judgement	Leverage one's knowledge
(Adapted from Dessler, 2001, pp. 109-115)	

Maxwell (2003);
Maxwell (2009)

Maxwell's Prescription. He researched how successful people *think*, and contends changing your thinking may "revolutionize your work," and by inference, your decisions. He writes, "The Right Thought plus the Right People in the Right Environment at the Right Time for the Right Reason equals the Right Result" (p. 18). His formula is supplemented with an eleven-function qualitative process for managers to employ. To conclude, when decision-makers fail to adjust their thinking, as proposed by Maxwell, and do not systematically evaluate, question, or research decision consequences, policy implementation may become problematic. Such was arguably the case for WF and VW.   WF: Absent   VW: Absent

Big-Picture Thinking

Focused Thinking   Reflective Thinking

Creative Thinking   Shared Thinking

Realistic Thinking   Bottom-Line Thinking

Strategic Thinking

Maxwell, J. C. (2009). *How successful people think: Change your thinking, change your life.* Boston, MA: Center Street. Copyright © 2009. Reprinted by permission from Center Street, an imprint of Hachette Books Group, Inc.

Combining, *realistic, shared, and strategic thinking* may have resulted in more people-focused WF and VW decisions.   WF: Absent   VW: Absent

---

Maxwell's Prescription for Decision Improvement
Consider these modes of thought:

Big-Picture

Focused   **Realistic**   **Shared**   **Strategic**

Creative   **Reflective**   **Bottom-line**

(Adapted from Maxwell, 2003, 2009)

(Financial egoism: an original definition)
Basu (2014);
Lockie (2015);
Quinn (2018);
Rockoff and Silverman (2016)

Financial egoism, coined by the author, refers to an individual, group, or organization's financial gain without regard for others who may be monetarily, physically, emotionally, or socially disadvantaged in some way. When this condition exists, it probably speaks to the root motivations of those who benefit. Financial egoism cases are frequent: Nestlé Bottled Water over pumping, 2015; Allan Stanford (Stanford Fin. Gr.) Ponzi scheme, 2009; and Valeant Pharmaceuticals price gouging, 2015. These cases garnered strong interest because of their egregious nature. How could this happen? One possibility may be obstacles to financial regulation of Ponzi schemes (Basu, 2014). To conclude, difficult to believe both storied companies WF and VW, and those above, would make decisions apparently rooted in financial egoism. Apparently, no strong devil's advocate present.   WF: Present   VW: Present

Kohlberg (1969);
Wells Fargo Online (2019)

Kohlberg's moral development and reasoning may also offer understanding regarding the subject execs' decisions. In this renowned longitudinal study of young boys, he theorized there are six stages of moral development and reasoning. Of interest here are Stages Five and Six, in which motivations focus on one's true concern for other persons' rights and one's greater concern for higher moral and ethical principles, respectively, such as, the bank's efforts to assist customers affected by the 2019 US government shutdown. To conclude, had the WF and VW execs embraced these stages caring about one's rights and adhering to ethical principles, their decisions would have benefited customers, employees, and other stakeholders. Problematic decisions would have been non-existent.   WF: Absent   VW: Absent

Boehmer (2001);
Boddy (2011);
Lashinsky (2019);
Tipgos (2002);
Verschool (2002);
Werhane et al. (2014)

Ethical counterviews contradict the notion that ethics training, codes of conduct, open communication, and ethics hotlines result in ethical cultures. Notable counterviews argue that ethical blind spots, management fraud, public malfeasance, and corporate psychopaths will continue making unethical decisions. Lashinsky's (2019) article describes evidence of execs behaving badly. To conclude, if the counterviews are credible, WF and VW exec decisions were intentional and perhaps motivated by financial egoism and competitive pressures. Apparently, no strong devil's advocate present. This is the human "X" factor, when decisions made are counter to that which was logically prudent and expected.

WF: Present   VW: Present

Daft (2016);
McKinsey and Company (2009);
Pfeffer and Sutton (2006)

Evidence-based management (EBM) refers to a more systematic process using questions in order to make knowledgeable decisions based on facts. EBM seeks facts. EBM sounds somewhat close to Domains of Decision Management (DDM), that is, there being an effort to produce meaningful and relevant required information on which to make decisions. In addition, DDM mandates a repetitive systematic and more structured evaluating, questioning, and researching, via proactively communicating, integrating, coordinating, and collaborating. Further, minimal previous decision learning may have also played a part here. To conclude, this Literature Review found no information addressing or suggesting the extent to which EBM questioning and scrutiny played a role in the WF or VW problematic decisions.

WF: Absent   VW: Absent

Birkinshaw et al. (2008); Ebert and Griffin (2015); Goldstein (2017); Higgins (1994); March and Simon (1958); Nieves (2016); Porter (1985); Russolillo and Bird (2018); Smith and Flanagan (2006); Steele (2018); TechTarget (2018)

Management innovation, one of four innovation types, refers to the implementation of new management policies, practices, procedures, or organizational structures to influence and have a direct effect on other types of innovation. The collective purposes of the above are the achievement of organizational goals and a competitive advantage. Service-oriented organizations (i.e., Google, AT&T, and Wegmans) continually invest in mgt innovation. CEO Roger Lynch of Pandora Media Inc., a music streaming firm, proclaimed, "Make sure you are always innovating" (p. R10). Other disciplines, such as high schools, colleges, and graduate schools, embrace management innovations. Educational management innovations are abundant in the U.S. especially in S-T-E-M instruction, and US graduate M.B.A. programs proliferate utilizing a combination of online, residency, and innovative robots. Germany's education systems maximize management innovations. March and Simon argued for organizational innovation. To conclude, the Literature Review did not locate any information indicating WF or VW utilized a structured management innovative decision-making process.

WF: Absent   VW: Absent

Daft (2016); McWhirter (2019)

Decision learning refers to *learning* from previous less effective decisions. If nothing is learned from a less effective decision, it could lessen decision quality in subsequent similar decisions. Significant learning resulted from Hurricane Katrina in 2005 that was evident in Hurricane Barry 2019; the upgraded levee system worked (McWhirter, 2019). To conclude, ideally, managers should analyze previous decisions for flaws and identify strategies to improve. Minimal decision learning may well have influenced WF and VW decisions resulting in problematic outcomes.

WF: Present   VW: Present

Brooks and Dunn
(2018);
Ferrell, Fraedrich, and
Ferrell (2019);
Kant (1788);
Mathews and Smith
(2015);
Xiong (2019)

Golden Rule-type decisions (GRTD). GRTD refers to a decision philosophy. In other words, how should senior management consider and care for employees, customers, and applicable stakeholders? GRTD is a belief that managerial decision-making should reflect the biblical *Golden Rule* that compels individuals to treat others the way they would like to be treated. GRTD demonstrate an excellent management stakeholder orientation.

Christianity's Sermon on the Mount in which Jesus commanded everyone to follow his teachings grounds GRTD philosophy. An a priori (preceding) Mosaic Law asserts, "Whatever is hurtful to you, do not do to any other man." In 1788, German philosopher Immanuel Kant published his *categorical imperative*, which states, "I ought never to act except in such a way that I can also will that my maxim should become a universal law (p. 144)."

The *Golden Rule* is considered the essence of morality, and is widely referenced in ethics textbooks assessing the ethicality of pending actions and decisions. Further, Roberts (2015) argues that servant leaders "Seek advice from a diverse group of knowledgeable and trustworthy sources to expand the scope of information, incorporate alternative views, and test their own assumptions" (p. 51). Similarly, all leaders should incorporate more diverse participative management.

For managers, GRTD would also exhibit the highest *Level of Strength* – Spiritual strength (Xiong, 2019). To conclude, GRTD decisions from WF and VW would have benefited all concerned.

WF: Absent   VW: Absent

Macklin and Mathison (2018);
Michaelson (2018);
Yin (2018)

Innovative Ethics Training. Macklin and Mathison (2018) recommended an academic community approach to developing business ethicists. They believe business ethicists should be reflexive in practice when instructing and consulting with practitioners and managers. A benefit would include collaboration with educators on more meaningful pedagogical techniques. These researchers argue their approach has more effectiveness than traditional grand theories of ethics or more focused theories of business ethics. They concluded their approach might be more grounded, and more practical and useful to ethics instructors, future business ethicists, and business practitioners.

Michaelson's (2018) creative thoughts are different, but certainly have potential. Great novelists possess power – having the ability to shape societal thought, psychological attitudes, behaviors, and to make life worth living, [or not worth living]. Narrative pedagogical methods are very useful in teaching business students, but the same methods do not seem practical for real-world businesses; claiming such an investment is not worth the time. However, some novels are beneficial enough to turn business students into better business people. Michaelson believes that certain novels cross the intersection of "what to do and how to live," which is what business employees and managers need to develop as people and professionals.

To conclude, both views are innovative. Macklin and Mathison argue that the best pedagogical techniques are practical, and useful to ethics instructors, future business ethicists, and business practitioners. Michaelson challenges business academics to embrace appropriate novels [also podcasts, TED Talks, and TV shows such as *American Greed*] in instructor curricula, referred to as *teaching-practices case studies* (Yin 2018). Both training approaches may have prevented the problematic decisions.   WF: Absent   VW: Absent

Collective Case Study (CCS) Qualitative Comparative Analysis (QCA) Matrix: How QCA Functions

QCA uses a small number of cases. Even though Wells Fargo and VW experienced decision factor similarities, each case is viewed as a combination of influencing factors linked to the decision outcomes. Next, the researcher examines each case and determines whether influencing factors and outcomes are either *present* or *absent*, thus producing a matrix specifying the configurations of causes that produced the outcomes.

Influencing Factors	QCA Evaluation: Present	QCA Evaluation: Absent
1. Enactment Theory	WF: Present VW: Present	
2. Positive Org. Culture		WF: Absent VW: Absent
3. Decision Environment	WF: Present VW: Present	
4. Bounded Rationality	WF: Present VW: Present	
5. Paradox of Choice		WF: Absent VW: Absent
6. Decision Process Failure (Any Decision Process)	WF: Present VW: Present	
7. Carnegie Model Alliances & Coalitions)	WF: Present VW: Present	
8. Garbage-Can		WF: Absent VW: Absent
9. Corporate Governance Failure	WF: Present VW: Present	
10. Groupthink	WF: Present VW: Present	

Influencing Factors	QCA Evaluation: Present	QCA Evaluation: Absent
11. In Search of Excellence		WF: Absent VW: Absent
12. Six Domains of Leadership		WF: Absent VW: Absent
13. Dessler's Prescription		WF: Absent VW: Absent
14. Maxwell's Prescription		WF: Absent VW: Absent
15. Financial Egoism	WF: Present VW: Present	
16. Kohlberg's Moral Dev.		WF: Absent VW: Absent
17. Ethical Counterviews	WF: Present VW: Present	
18. Evidence-Based Mgt.		WF: Absent VW: Absent
19. Mgt. Innovation		WF: Absent VW: Absent
20. Minimal Decision Learning	WF: Present VW: Present	
21. Golden Rule-Type Decisions		WF: Absent VW: Absent
22. Innovative Ethics Training		WF: Absent VW: Absent
Totals:	10	12
CCS: VW:	10 Presents	12 Absents
CCS: WF:	10 Presents	12 Absents

Influencing Factors	QCA Evaluation: Present	QCA Evaluation: Absent

Five Most Likely Decision Factors	4, 6/20, 7, 9, 10
	    Each factor contributed to problematic decisions; the three-person expert panel subsequently determined the ordering of the five likely factors. A random ordering follows below.
	    The five are bounded rationality, decision process failure and minimal decision learning, the Carnegie model (coalition and alliance groupings), corporate governance failure, and groupthink.	

* Adapted from discussion of qualitative comparative analysis and the researcher's role: Bernard & Ryan, (2010) (For a very brief introduction to the method); Ragin & Amoroso, (2011) (For a slightly longer but accessible introduction to the method by its originator, Ragin); Rhioux & Lobe discuss QCA in B. Byrne & C. C. Ragin, Eds. (2009). *Handbook of Cross-Case Methods.* London, England: Sage; and Rhioux & Ragin, (2009), (as cited in Schwandt, 2015, p. 255).

Table 5 combines induction findings and quantitative treatment of five likely decision factors. There were: 1) combinations of decision factors; 2) slightly differing decision environments; however, the slightly different decision environments produced near similar problematic decision outcomes regarding the effects on people, financials, ethical standing, and organizational reputations.

Literature Review Summary

Based on the CCS Qualitative Comparative Analysis (QCA), the researcher presents five likely factors influencing Wells Fargo and VW decisions. See the five most probable influencing factors below, in no particular order:

- Bounded Rationality. Decision-makers suffered from the cognitive limitation of bounded rationality, a limited capacity to process information, a disadvantage from the start.

- Decision Process Failure and Minimal Decision Learning. A decision process, quasirationality, evidence-based, or a rational one, failed perhaps because of ill-weighted criteria, insufficient facts, or minimal previous decision learning that refers to decision-makers learning from previous less effective decisions. In such a case, decision outcomes would be suboptimal.

- Carnegie Model. Internal alliances and coalitional pressures were acting on managers who were pressed to match or exceed the competition.

- Groupthink. Often groups make decisions to maintain group harmony rather than selecting a more examined and capable option.

- Corporate Governance Failure. Perhaps the most impactful likely factor were Wells Fargo and VW corporate governance failures of their Board of Directors and Board of Supervisors, respectively. The Boards failed in their fiduciary responsibility to protect the companies from financial and reputational risk.

Subsequently, a three-person expert panel further examined these five factors with differing opinions and positioning. See the five most likely influencing factors' final ordering in Table 5.

7 Research Approaches

This chapter discusses, to some level of detail, three research methodologies. First, a collective case study (CCS) to obtain evidence regarding the Wells Fargo and VW problematic decision outcomes. Second, the first qualitative study to obtain findings and themes regarding Domains of Decision Management (DDM) capabilities. Third, a second qualitative study to obtain findings and themes regarding the Wells Fargo and VW problematic decision outcomes, and last, a quantitative study to obtain the Pearson's r product-moment correlation coefficient, and the strength and direction of the DDM variables. Discussions follow.

Collective Case Study (CCS) Component

The research documents, the semi-structured interviews, the direct observations, and the expert panel resulted in a convergence of data and evidence, which according to Yin (2018), strengthened construct validity, also producing sufficient evidence to differentiate case similarities, differences, and analytic generalizations. The CCS evidence linked to conclusions via induction, a strategy of collecting loads of relevant evidence and then inferring a general conclusion. (Schwandt, 2015). Since the researcher did not personally witness the Wells Fargo or VW decisions, this study researched likely factors influencing the Wells Fargo and VW decisions, as recommended by Yin (2018). Collective case study was necessary because it:

- Allows for two cases to be researched simultaneously

- Allows for understanding likely factors about specific Wells Fargo (WF) and VW decisions

- Generates knowledge about WF and VW decisions, where the researcher had no control

- Describes what kinds of actions this collective case study is about

- Uses qualitative comparative analysis (QCA), a type of comparative case method, and a type of cross-case method

- Allows for knowing collective case similarities and differences

- Allows for use of data triangulation and theory triangulation

- Allows for making comparisons, and

- Allows for multiple case study analytic generalizations (restricted to automobile executives)

Data and theory triangulation were essential in making sense of the evidence in this collective case study (Ragin, 2014; Ragin & Becker, 1992; Schwandt, 2015; Stake, 1995; Yin, 2018)

Qualitative Component

A qualitative study was necessary because little was known about Wells Fargo and VW decision environments. This research approach was appropriate because it:

- Is often used to gather background information when little is known about the topic

- Recognizes the researcher as the key instrument

- Allows for a better understanding of the dependent, independent, and mediating variable relationships; although *vari-*

ables, in their traditional sense, are a major topic of debate in case study literature (See Ragin, 2014; Yin, 2018)

- Allows for data triangulation and occurs in the respondent's natural setting

- Allows for a convergence of evidence, and

- Creates emergent categories, meanings, and themes

(Creswell, 2013; Creswell, 2014; Leedy & Ormrod, 2019; Sekaran & Bougie, 2016)

Quantitative Component

Functional characteristics of quantitative inquiry include deductive reasoning, theory testing, rigor, replicability, and objective measure. A quantitative component was needed to:

- Test the DDM theory regarding its dependent, independent, and mediating variables

- Confirm and validate study findings, allowing for inferences

- Analyze with parametric statistics to obtain the Pearson's *r* product moment correlation coefficient (Creswell, 2013; Creswell, 2014; Leedy & Ormrod, 2019).

To conclude, these three research components, over a three-year period, have coalesced to produce findings that provided clarity into the Wells Fargo and VW decision environments. Both company environments were essentially bombarded with management pressure to match or exceed their competitors.

8 Research Methods

Sample: Knowledgeable Respondents

The DDM qualitative and quantitative sample included 33 individuals in which individuals and groups of individuals were asked to participate in a single-item, dual-purpose questionnaire. They were advised they would remain anonymous, and in a following discussion, each provided his or her verbal approval. Having these approvals, data collection began as respondents willingly entered qualitative data into a Comments Box, and indicated the quantitative degree to which they believed the DDM was beneficial (Leedy & Ormrod, 2019). All individuals were *knowledgeable respondents.*

These DDM knowledgeable respondents included a heterogeneous purposive sampling of university undergraduates, graduate management, public administration, and M.B.A. students in mid to late 30s. There were 17 students with an average age of 37.5 years. If each began working at age 22, each had 15.5 years of adult working experience. Thus, their total approximate years decision-making and observing managerial decisions and consequences were 263.5. Two school staff members added 31 years of decision-making and observing the consequences of managerial decisions.

Additionally, there were 14 local city business owners and managers, the Chamber of Commerce members, plus the city Mayor. The age range of these individuals was the mid-'30s to early '40s, approximately 40. One variable remaining the same was beginning work at age 22. Thus, the years of adults working were 40 – 22 = 18. Therefore, total years of these 14 individuals' decision-making and employees having years observing the consequences of managerial decisions were 252.

While this total sample of 33 may be perceived as small, it is argued that the test item responses were the result of 263.5 + 31 + 252 = 546.5 years of hands-on decision-making experiences and employees observing the consequences of managerial decisions. Five hundred forty-six point five years (546.5) of decision making experiences and observing the consequences of managerial decisions is no small matter and should be complimented and recognized.

The DDM quantitative sample of 33 was small. For that reason, the researcher made no claims to generalize the findings to any larger population. *Representativeness bias* refers to making such a generalization (Jones & George, 2014). However, from a qualitative perspective, this is a workable sample. Leedy and Ormrod (2019), for qualitative phenomenological samples, argue a minimum sample of five (5) as being workable, provided knowledgeable respondents participate. (The data saturation point occurred at about the 25th respondent).

Accepting this point of view, the researcher contends DDM qualitative respondents' test item responses resulted from 263.5 + 31 + 252 = 546.5 years of practical decision-making experiences and employees observing the consequences of managerial decisions, which carries more evaluative weight than a small quantitative sample. The researcher interpreted 546.5 years as research significant.

To capture this significance, the researcher developed this factor to recognize any small sample's years of valid work experience. The term Respondent Experience Factor (REF), coined here, gives significant weight to collective work experiences, rather than easily forgotten small sample sizes.

To determine the REF, see below examples:

Step 1. Obtain each respondent's current age. For example, 41

a. For each respondent, obtain the age he or she began working. For example, age 18

b. Employee. Subtract working age from his or her current age: $41 - 18 = 23$ years work experience

c. Manager or supervisor (MoS). MoS may have two ages to compute, manager years and employee years. For a 40 year old who began work at 22, her employee years may be 15; her manager years are 25.

d. Total all employee respondents' years + all MoS employees' years + all MoS managers' years = the Respondent Experience Factor (REF)

Step 2. For age sensitive individuals, those who select an age group, for example,40-45.

a. Determine the average age of that group, $40+41+42+43+44+45 = 255/6 = 42.5$ years.

b. Subtract their working age from his or her current average age: $42.5 - 20 = 22.5$ years work experience

c. Total all in this category.

d. Grand total: Sum all Step 1 employees and managers and, all Step 2 employees and managers = the Respondent Experience Factor for that research.

Data Collection

The collective case study (CCS) included Wells Fargo District level and below management interviews. A District manager and seven Wells Fargo Branch managers offered their recovery perspectives via face-to-face and telephone interviews. Workplace observations were helpful. Similarly, VW interviews included five VW Sales managers and one VW Repair Shop owner, with workplace observations.

Moreover, a review of open-source documents was comprehensive. All CCS respondents were candid as they described how their organizations were regaining and gaining the trust of current and potential customers. The below questions are consistent with Yin's position that substantive questions collect evidence (2018). See Table 4 and Appendix A for Wells Fargo and VW respondents' themes and interview discussions.

DDM Research and CCS Protocol Questions

- **Q1.** CCS. What kinds of actions describe this collective case study?

- **Q2.** CCS. What kinds of actions describe the collective case study similarities?

- **Q3.** CCS. What kinds of actions describe the collective case study differences?

- **Q4.** CCS. What kinds of actions describe the collective case study analytic generalizations?

- **Q5a, b.** CCS. What kinds of actions is this dealership (or Repair Shop) [and senior management] doing to regain and gain the trust of current and potential VW customers?

- **Q6a, b.** CCS. What kinds of actions is this Wells Fargo Branch [and senior management] doing to regain and gain the trust of current and potential customers?

- **Q7.** CCS. What are the five most likely factors influencing the Wells Fargo and VW problematic decisions?

- **Q8.** DDM. Based on your workplace experiences as a decision-maker or as a management observer:

  To what degree do you believe a decision process that assists managers in determining (i.e., subjectively and objectively) the impact of potential decisions on people, time, financials, the organization, and moral and ethical implications, may be beneficial?

No benefit	Little benefit	Neutral	Above-average benefit	Very beneficial
1	2	3	4	5

Comment briefly on the above approach to decision making:

9 Research Findings

Collective Case Study Questions

- **Q1.** CCS. What kinds of actions describe this collective case study? See Collective Case Study Research Findings.

- **Q2.** CCS. What kinds of actions describe the collective case study similarities? See Collective Case Study Research Findings.

- **Q3.** CCS. What kinds of actions describe the collective case study differences? See Collective Case Study Research Findings.

- **Q4.** CCS. What kinds of actions describe the collective case study analytic generalizations? See Collective Case Study Research Findings.

Interview Themes, Likely Decision Factors

- **Q5a.** CCS. What kinds of actions is this dealership (or Repair Shop) doing to regain and gain the trust of current and potential VW customers? See Table 4 and Appendix D.

- **Q6a.** CCS. What kinds of actions is this Wells Fargo Branch doing to regain and gain the trust of current and potential customers? See Table 4 and Appendix D.

- **Q7.** CCS. What are the five most likely factors influencing the Wells Fargo and VW problematic decisions? See Table 5.

Domains of Decision Management Qualitative Themes and Quantitative Scatter Plot

- **Q8.** DDM. Based on your workplace experiences as a decision-maker or as a management observer:

    To what degree do you believe a decision process that assists managers in determining (i.e., subjectively and objectively) the impact of potential decisions on people, time, financials, the organization, and moral and ethical implications, may be beneficial?

No benefit	Little benefit	Neutral	Above-average benefit	Very beneficial
1	2	3	4	5

Comment briefly on the above approach to decision making:

See Table 6 and Figure 4.

Collective Case Study Research Findings

Q1. What kinds of actions describe this collective case study? Research evidence created a portrait indicating human cognitive limitations, corporate governance failures, coalitions and alliances, sociological groupthink, decision process failure and minimal decision learning, most likely influenced Wells Fargo and VW decision practitioners.

Q2. What kinds of actions describe the collective case study similarities? 1) Both companies were major corporations, 2) Both corporate governance charters included similar terms stressing risk management, maintaining corporate integrity, and maintaining an ethical culture. Also, 3) Both Boards failed in their fiduciary responsibilities to protect the company from financial harm, and 4) Presently, both companies are exerting positive efforts to regain and gain customer trust.

Q3. What kinds of actions describe the collective case study differences? 1) One bank, one automaker. 2) The VW two-week communications lapse between *clean diesel* managers and the 20-member Board of Supervisors was perhaps intentional. 3) The VW culture was termed corrupted (Gates, Keller, Russell, & Watkins, 2015; VAP, 2018). 4) Wells Fargo's unethical culture was troubling because the company has historically been trustworthy; recovery from this scandal has extended into 2019 (Clozel & Ackerman, 2019), and 2020. 5) The VW actions and behaviors to regain customer trust are more visible and effectual because dealership Sales and Service Management established immediate face-to-face working relationships with irritated *clean diesel* customers, and, for the most part, reduced customer irritation sooner rather than later. 6) In contrast, Wells Fargo's duty of regaining and gaining potential customer trust, to this researcher, is perceived as more difficult to accomplish because customer information was manipulated in a clandestine fashion; this was egregious and unknown to customers, but strongly favored by banking executives.

Q4. What kinds of actions describe the collective case study analytic generalizations? 1) Both companies should increase executive ethics training. 2) Both companies should increase Board ethics training. 3) Both companies should establish clear parameters when senior executives must inform their Board on key strategic business and operational decisions. 4) Ensure both companies initiate a formal decision-making process that maximizes *Golden Rule*-type decisions, where consideration of internal employees, external customers and stakeholder relationships are valued. These actions would exhibit an excellent management stakeholder orientation.

Table 4

Collective Case Study Volkswagen and Wells Fargo Interview Qualitative Themes

---

Q5a. CCS. What kinds of actions is this dealership (or Repair Shop) doing to regain and gain the trust of current and potential VW customers? See Appendices A and D.

Volkswagen qualitative themes (Actions or behaviors appear in italics)

- **Customer Service:** VW *Ambassadors* are certified and dedicated to customer satisfaction
- *Customer Satisfaction* is #1; Service Managers must reason with customers *regardless of customer temperament*
- *Friendliness* toward customers; *take care of the customer, first*
- Be *honest* and *transparent; provide expert customer service*
- Sales and Service: *make it personal;* exhibit a *customer first attitude*
- Believe in *going above-and-beyond*
- **Quality and Learning:** *Quality* is *attention to detail; know customer vehicles well*
- *Lessons in humanity* learned by all
- Sales staff *temperament appeared affable and ready for action*
- **Altruism:** *Corporate social responsibility* (CSR) is a big deal for multiple dealerships
- **Maximize Sells:** Dealerships buy stored vehicles, *install the upgrades, and produce a fully functional and certified VW used automobile.* Everyone wins.
- *Love the product*
  - ➤ These daily actions and behaviors go far in regaining and gaining customer trust.

Q6a. CCS. What kinds of actions is this Wells Fargo Branch doing to regain and gain the trust of current and potential customers? See Appendices A and D.

Wells Fargo Qualitative Themes: (Actions or behaviors appear in italics)

- **Customer Service:** Keep the *customer first;* strive to provide the best customer service; *demonstrate* customer service is *a top priority*
- *Be polite and respectful of customers*
- Recommend *periodic financial reviews*
- Be open to *address customers' concerns*
- Require Bankers and Tellers to *know their customers and build relationships*
- **Positive Environment:** Team members *working together; having positive working attitudes*
- Expect a *positive in-the-bank atmosphere*
- Allow team members *to voice their issues* and *opinions*
- **Altruism and Leadership:** *Be committed to one's leadership style,* such as: to be the leader you want to follow; teach and develop others; be passionate, and be ethical
- Be committed to the corporate leadership style: *Tell-Show-Do-Review*
- Make bold efforts to *participate in corporate social responsibility* (CSR)
- Maximize the *power of management collaboration*
- Disseminate *Important Information about the 2019 Government Shutdown*
- Ensure Tellers and Bankers have a *working knowledge of WF policies*
  - ➤ These daily actions and behaviors go far in regaining and gaining customer trust.

- **Q7. CCS. What are the five most likely factors influencing the Wells Fargo and VW problematic decisions?**

Table 5 combines induction findings and quantitative treatment of five likely decision factors. There were: 1) combinations of decision factors; 2) slightly differing decision environments; however, the slightly different decision environments produced near similar problematic decision outcomes regarding the effects on people, financials, ethical standing, and organizational reputations.

A three-person expert panel, which made arguments and repositioned the five decision factors, included the researcher and two decision-savvy colleagues, all doctoral-level.

Table 5

Five Most Likely Factors Influencing the Wells Fargo and Volkswagen Problematic Decisions

(Author/Researcher)	Step 1	Step 2		Peer Debriefer 1		Step 3
Corp. Gov. Failure (CGF):	1st	5+4=9		Carnegie Model (CM):	1st	5+3=8
Groupthink (GT):	2nd	4+3=7		a. Bounded Rationality(BR):2nd		4+5=9
Carnegie Model (CM):	3rd	3+5=8		Decision Process Failure &	3rd	3+0=3
Decision Process Failure & (DPF)				Minimal Decision Learning (DPF):		
Minimal Decision Learning:4th		0+3=3		Corp. Gov. Failure (CGF):	4th	0+5=5
Bounded Rationality (BR):	5th	0+5=5		Groupthink (GT):	5th	0+4=4

Peer Debriefer 2				Points (pts.)	
Bounded Rationality (BR):	1st	5+4=9		1st place	5pts
Corp. Gov. Failure (CGF):	2nd	4+5=9		2nd place	4pts
a. Groupthink (GT):	3rd	3+4=7		3rd place	3pts
Carnegie Model CM):	4th	0+5=5		4th place	0pts
Decision Process Failure & (DPF)				5th place	0pts
Minimal Decision Learning: 5th		0+3=3		Note: Places 1st - 3rd carry greater weight than places 4th - 5th for primary ratings.	

Highest sums and multiply x 2

Step 4	Five Most Likely Factors Influencing WF and VW Decisions
	Step 5
CGF 2x9 = 18	1st-2nd **Corporate Governance Failure (CGF)**
BR 2x9 = 18	1st-2nd **Bounded Rationality (BR)**
CM 2x8 = 16	3rd **Carnegie Model (CM)**
GT 2x7 = 14	4th **Groupthink (GT)**
DPF 2x3 = 6	5th **Decision Process Failure &**
	Minimal Decision Learning (DPF & MDL)

A three-person expert panel debated for repositioning the Literature Summary's five likely decision factors. **Step 1,** each panel member rates all five primary factors. **Step 2,** searches other Debriefers' ratings for similarly titled primary factors. After locating the same primary title with the highest rating, it was entered into his or her equation. For example, the 3 pts from Debriefer 2a, Groupthink, now appears in the Step 2 position of the researcher's second equation (4+3=7). The three panel members for all five primaries repeated this step. **Step 3,** sums each panel members' five separate equations. See Debriefer 1a's Bounded Rationality equation that shows its initial rating of 4 pts + 5 pts from Debriefer 2's first pts of 5, (4+5=9). **Step 4,** first identified the highest Step 3 sums, then multiplied them in decreasing order times 2. Notice some factors, for example, CGF and BR have two sums of 9 pts each; CM has two sums of 8 pts each, but only one of each factor is selected for Step 4. **Step 5,** enters the places first to 5th for each likely factor. There may be ties, as in this final computation. [See the value of expert panels in Sekaran and Bougie (2016)].

- **Q8. DDM. Based on your workplace experiences as a decision-maker or as a management observer:**

"To what degree do you believe a decision process that assists managers in determining (i.e., subjectively and objectively) the impact of potential decisions on people, time, financials, the organization, and moral and ethical implications, may be beneficial?"

No benefit	Little benefit	Neutral	Above-average benefit	Very beneficial
1	2	3	4	5

Comment briefly on the above approach to decision making:

Quantitative finding. A better understanding of the DDM model was attained. Thirty of 33 respondents (90.9%) believed there was potential for decision outcomes to range from above-average to very beneficial, provided the model is followed. The DDM scatter plot indicated a strong, positive Pearson r correlation coefficient of +0.96. As such, the study confirms and validates the inference that above-average to very beneficial decisions are achievable. See the scatter plot in Figure 4. A *Respondent Experience Factor* of 546.5 years was recognized.

Qualitative finding. The qualitative findings resulting from extensive time in the field, triangulation, and thick and rich respondent descriptions, produced prevalent and relevant emergent themes. From the DDM test instrument, four categories of themes emerged: One general decision-making category, and three specific to DDM. The DDM combined themes were educational and instructive. The DDM themes appear in Table 6 (Creswell, 2013/2014; Leedy & Ormrod, 2019). These themes were the product of 546.5 years of purposive individuals holding decision-making positions and employees observing the consequences of managerial decisions. The researcher, to recognize, to give weight to, and to represent the collective working years of purposive respondents, originated the Respondent Experience Factor (REF).

Several actions and procedures contributed to the credibility of these DDM and CCS findings. Data and theory triangulation of multiple data sources and extensive time in the field conducting interviews were most revealing. Respondents' thick descriptions describing their unique lived decision-making experiences and CCS experiences were central to these studies. WF Managers, VW Managers, a Shop owner, and knowledgeable respondents who observed the consequences of managerial decisions were excellent sources of information. Further, counterview data, as discussed, remains relevant to this day. Peer debriefings from university colleagues were invaluable. All the above contributed to this study's construct validity (Creswell, 2014; Leedy & Ormrod, 2019).

Qualitative findings emerged via Creswell's Data Analysis Spiral (2013). Analysis utilized four reliable steps: Organizing the data; Perusal; Classification; and Synthesis, integrating and summarizing the data. The DDM themes emerged via open coding producing four categories (Leedy & Ormrod, 2019). See Table 6.

Table 6

Decision Making and Domains of Decision Management (DDM) Qualitative Themes

---

General Decision-Making Qualitative Themes

*Decisions in General. A thorough brainstorming process to formulate ideas makes for a positive approach to decision-making.
*A decision-making process is an essential function that directly reflects the bottom line.
*Look before you leap or speak. Listen first. [This is an inference to examine thoroughly and listen to advisors when making decisions].
*In all decision-making processes, take all the time given and go through every step.

   ➤ Brainstorm thoroughly, listen carefully, be creative, and use all available time.

Domains of Decision Management (DDM)© Qualitative Themes

*Being Innovative. It is innovative and new.
*It is an important model that is teachable across all levels of management.
*DDM has the capability to align organizational culture toward cohesive ethical awareness and decision-making.
*DDM may assist in evaluating moral and ethical issues.
*It is important for managers to have a decision process when thinking about the various impacts [i.e., negative or positive] any potential decision may have.

*Essential Factors. The factors covered in this decision-making approach [i.e., people, time, financials, the organization, and morals and ethics] are central to the DDM process.
*Taking these factors [i.e., the people, time, financials, the organization, and morals and ethics] into consideration is vital for a successful organization.
*Organizations and teams are made up of people, [dealing with: time, financials, the organization, and moral and ethical implications] so anything that guides a manager in a positive direction is beneficial.

*Structure and Process. Successful decisions depend on a systematic process.
*DDM gives decision-makers parameters (i.e., a thing, which decides, or limits the way in which something is done) from which to act.
*It is essential to balance DDM subjectivity (S) and objectivity (O) in the Worksheets, when condition descriptors are plentiful; otherwise S and O balance may not be possible.
*If a DDM step is skipped or relevant information not considered, it may negatively affect the decision outcome.

   ➤ DDM has the capability to produce above-average to very beneficial decisions resulting in more sustainable business practices, when all DDM procedures are followed.

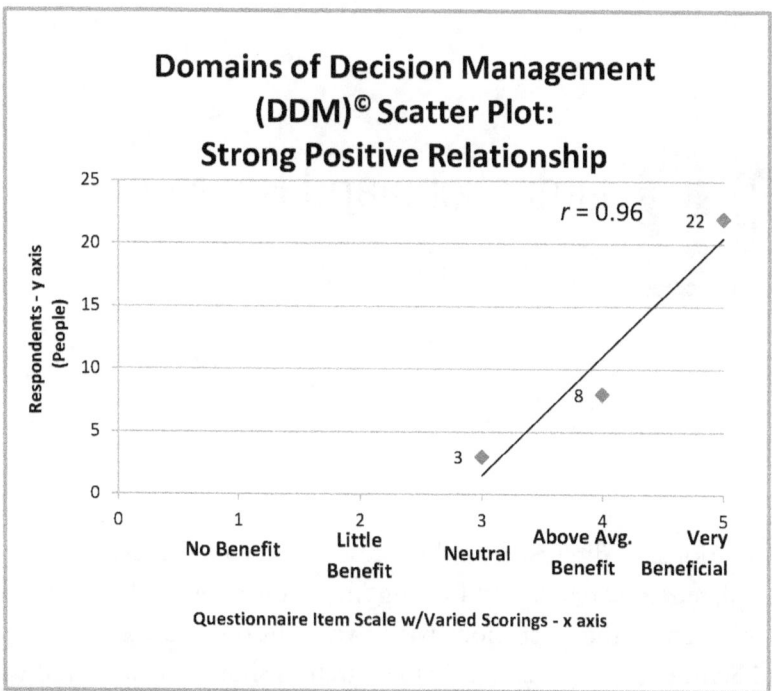

Figure 4. Domains of Decision Management[©] Scatter Plot. This graphic describes the relationship between variables. When measured via an interval scale, computing a correlation coefficient indicates the *strength* and *direction* of the relationship between the variables. The most frequently used measure of association in determining correlation is the Pearson product-moment correlation coefficient, commonly referred to as the Pearson *r*. The Pearson *r* ranges from -1 to +1.

The DDM Scatter Plot indicates a *strong positive relationship,* shown by its *line-of-best-fit.* The calculated Pearson *r* linear correlation coefficient is + 0.96.

This strong relationship permits a researcher to appreciate the line-of-best-fit and allows for *predictions* based on the data. However, strong correlation coefficients do not suggest or infer a *causal* relationship. Groundings: (Creswell, 2013/2014; Leedy & Ormrod, 2019; Sekaran & Bougie, 2016).

10 Limitations and Research Opportunities

Limitations, as discussed by these researchers, refer to evaluating the completed research by addressing three questions. The researcher supplemented the discussions with two additional questions. Cooper and Schindler (2011) assert that researchers should be open and candid in addressing limitations and other revealing information.

Did the Planned Procedures Compare to the Actual Procedures?

Yes. The procedures were consistent with standard case study, qualitative and quantitative studies. The subsequent Wells Fargo (2018) and VW (2019) business strategies were senior management's corporate updates, advising on current and planned management re-organizations. See Appendix D.

Did the Planned Sample Compare to the Actual Sample?

Yes. As stated, the 33 respondents completed the qualitative and quantitative questionnaire. The CCS sample included case study interviews with seven Wells Fargo Branch managers, one District manager, five VW Sales managers, and one VW Repair Shop owner. Particular attention guided the researcher's selection of purposive, knowledgeable individuals. This researcher concluded all Wells Fargo and VW respondents were well versed in their responsibilities and understood organization leadership. All respondents were open and candid in their descriptions about how their organizations were regaining and gaining the trust of current and potential customers.

Was There an Impact on Findings and Conclusions?

Perhaps a miniscule percentage of students felt obligated to support the instructor's DDM model. However, the researcher believed most students responded to the questionnaire in an individual and honest manner. Researcher bias was withheld to prevent influencing respondent responses on DDM capabilities; all Wells Fargo and VW respondents spoke freely and openly describing their efforts to regain and gain the trust of current and potential customers. The 33 DDM knowledgeable respondents were candid in their Comment Box qualitative statements and in responding to the quantitative test item. The collective case study findings presented themselves during data analysis.

The researcher derived the Respondent Experience Factor (REF) that gives credence and weight to the collective work experiences of respondents, rather than disregarding small qualitative and quantitative samples as inferior. In other words, REF respects the collective work experiences of knowledgeable respondents. Subject to this discussion is deriving an acceptable minimum of collective working years. This researcher recommends a 50-year minimum.

What Will the Sixth Likely Decision Factor Be?

Theologians may argue in favor of financial egoism as the sixth or higher decision factor. According to the Apostle Paul, all wrongdoing results from excessive material wealth. Stated succinctly, "Money is the root of all evil," Apostle Paul (as cited in Hirsch, Kett, & Trefil, 2002, p. 53).

Business ethicists' may argue in favor of unbridled greed as the sixth or higher decision factor. According to the Literature Review, ethical counterviews, ethical blind spots, management fraud, public malfeasance, and corporate psychopaths will continue making questionable and unethical decisions (Boddy, 2011; Lashinsky, 2019; Tipgos, 2002; Verschool, 2002; and Werhane et al., 2014).

Is This a Longitudinal Wells Fargo and VW study?

Ensign (2019) reported, regarding bank human resource issues, the Office of the Comptroller of the Currency (OCC) regulator insists there are still "matters requiring attention" (p. A8). Ensign and Kellaher (2019) reported that Wells Fargo's legal Counsel, C. Allen Parker, will leave his position on or about March 31, 2020. (Ensign & Kellaher, as cited in Dow Jones Newswires (2019, November 15).

Equally important, Wells Fargo, in a February 21, 2020, legal settlement, agreed to pay $3 billion to resolve government investigations by the US Justice Department and the Securities and Exchange Commission (SEC) for its cross-sells scandal and other charges. Prosecutors said the cross-sells practices date to 1998 when an apparent business strategy changed. The US attorney in Los Angeles, CA, concluded, "Wells Fargo traded its hard-earned reputation for short-term profits" (Eisen, 2020, pp. A1, A10). Although not fully exonerated, this was good news for the beleaguered bank. Separately, the Office of the Comptroller of the Currency recently charged eight former Wells Fargo executives over the cross-sells scandal (Eisen, 2020). Legal cases are ongoing.

Wells Fargo's new CEO, Charlie Scharf, testifying before a US House Finance Committee, March 10, 2020, acknowledged, "The sense of urgency within the company is very different today than it was four months ago." He stressed that he spends 75% of his time on regulatory issues. Continuing, he asserted, "We are going to have a much stronger centralized core when it comes to risk and control" (Levitt & Dexheimer, 2020).

Volkswagen-in-Australia was recently fined $125 million for the emissions scandal. A separate finance-related lawsuit is pending (Reuters, 2019). Volkswagen AG recently reported that some China VW

Plants would stay closed due to employee transportation and plant logistics issues caused by the Coronavirus pandemic (Moss, 2020). This collective case study (CCS) may be longitudinal.

Research Opportunities

Researchers working individually or in teams are invited to conduct expanded collective case studies, qualitative, and quantitative studies. A mixed-methods study is perceived as the research approach capable of obtaining a more thorough perspective of Domains of Decision Management capabilities. The 33 respondents supporting the qualitative and quantitative components of this study should be exceeded. According to Creswell (2014), utilize separate sample individuals for the qualitative and quantitative components. Managers should benefit from a mixed-methods study (Creswell, 2014; Leedy & Ormrod, 2019).

Two levels of *action research*, which refers to "a research strategy aimed at initiating change processes, with an incremental focus, for narrowing the gap between the desired and actual states," (Sekaran & Bougie, 2016, p. 389) are recommended in the Schools of Business and Management: Master's and Doctoral.

Master's: Conduct qualitative *action research* on an actual organization for 13 to 14 weeks at the branch and division level. The respondents at this level would be a collective minimum of eight (8) supervisors and mid-level managers. This DDM evaluation occurs at either the Informal (IF) or Single-Person (SP) level. The Probability Decision Committee (PDC) is formed for these evaluations.

Doctoral: For a more comprehensive and involved qualitative action research project, this level first recognizes the seminal work of Rensis Likert, in his book, *New Patterns of Management* (1961), that posits "larger organizations should expect to take appreciably longer than smaller organizations in shifting their operations (i.e., decision making) to the newer theory," (pp. 245-246), (it is the Domains of Decision Management theory). Respondents at this unit of analysis should be the most senior managers in the organization: Chief Executive Officer, President, Chief Operations Officer, Chief Finance Officer, Board Chairman, and Sales Managers. At least seven or more Vice Presidents should be included. The respondents at this level would be a collective minimum of twelve (12) individuals. A minimum time for this research project is six (6) months. The Probability Decision Committee (PDC) is formed. This DDM evaluation occurs at either the Formal (F) or Informal (IF) level, the recommended level is Formal.

In both cases, the researcher would be the DDM coordinator, to withhold biases, interact with respondents, and advise as needed. Such research would entail:

- Selecting an organization and receiving approval for the research

- Adopting DDM Assumptions as discussed in this report.

- Defining DDM as a *prescriptive management-centered decision-making process* to all participating in the research, which includes forming the *Probabilities Decision Committee* (PDC).

- Making common knowledge the DDM philosophy: 1) improving the quality of managerial decisions, 2) reiterating potential benefits of DDM decisions, and 3) instilling the company mantra, "DDM: Decisions with principles."

- Defining the five Domains: *people, time, financials,* the *organization,* and *moral* and *ethical* impacts. See **Nature of the Domains**

- Monitoring the DDM operative actions of *evaluating, questioning,* and *researching* problems, issues, and opportunities via the processes of *proactive communication, integration, coordination,* and *collaboration*

Initially, develop *condition descriptors* similar to the organization's verbiage; this aligns DDM language with that of the test organization, reducing the learning curve. See *action research* in Leedy and Ormrod (2019), Mills (2018), and Sekaran & Bougie (2016).

11 Recommendations and Conclusion

Table 7

Recommendations to Organizational Leadership

Domains of Decision Management© Recommendations to Organizational Leadership. Senior Leaders should:

- Institutionalize Domains of Decision Management (DDM)© as a management innovation integrating it into the organization's strategic decision-making process and embracing *Golden Rule*-type decisions. To do so demonstrates excellent stakeholder management orientation.

- Establish DDM as a management-centered process. Senior management is responsible for introducing, training, implementing, maintaining, and establishing DDM as a management innovation.

- Establish a three-person Probabilities Decision Committee (PDC) to consider and determine Probabilities of Occurrence (PO) as a functional element in the DDM Worksheet. Vice Presidents, at a minimum, are recommended; these individuals must be well versed in organizational operations, risk management, and company priorities.

- Establish ethics and decision process training for senior corporate managers, Boards of Directors, and Supervisors that emphasizes timely coordinated decisions and the importance of adhering to a structured DDM process.

- Establish DDM with an evaluative component in performance appraisals. Evaluate managers, annually, on their degree of DDM use and its effectiveness.

- Ensure DDM proactive communication, integration, coordination, and collaboration, act in a *process* role supporting the *operative* evaluating, questioning, and researching with maximum collective work effort.

- Maximize the usefulness of *decision information* by increasing its *quality* (i.e., accurate and reliable), *timeliness* (i.e., current and up-to-date), *completeness* (i.e., all that is needed), and *relevance* (i.e., related to the matter at hand).

Table 8
Recommendations to Wells Fargo and Volkswagen Leadership

Wells Fargo and Volkswagen Leadership

Leaders should:

- **Value Decision Learning.** Gain valuable knowledge from previous less successful decisions, and apply that learning to future decisions.

- **Conduct Company Training.** Conduct executive level and Board training to reinforce company values and fiduciary responsibilities. Instill company values as stated in Wells Fargo's *Business Standards Report* (Dec. 2018), and VW's Strategy *Together 2025+* (VW, 2019).

- **Make Structured Decisions.** Initiate a formal decision-making process that maximizes Domains of Decision Management tenets and *Golden Rule*-type decisions (GRTD), where consideration of employees, customers, and stakeholder relationships are valued.

- **Initiate Corporate Social Responsibility (CSR).** Projects such as awarding $500 college academic scholarships to alternating high school graduating seniors. This CSR initiative would demonstrate management's support to local students. [Interviews with both company managers found a real desire to give back to their local communities]

Conclusion

March and Simon established the urgency of institutionalizing organizational innovation (1958). This research has argued on behalf of the institutionalization of the Domains of Decision Management

(DDM) as a management innovation. The DDM model posits that managers may achieve above-average to very beneficial decisions by systematically evaluating, questioning, and researching five interdependent management Domains – people, time, financials, the organization, and moral and ethical implications. Drucker (1966) endorsed decisions emanating from a systematic process having clearly defined elements and a sequence of steps, which the DDM possesses. To maximize DDM benefits, management's commitment to its theoretical tenets must be unwavering.

Both companies made problematic decisions. Subsequent evidence, VW Strategy Together 2025+, asserts VW undertaking a multiyear project reforming corporate governance, decentralizing decision making, using decarburization index to make CO2 targets measurable, and communicating with all stakeholders to regain and further build trust (VW.com, 2019). VW interviews confirmed dealerships committed to service. Subsequent Wells Fargo management advised it is improving the company culture, reorganizing the Board of Directors, eliminating product sales goals, and instituting stronger management oversight. See Appendix D.

Wells Fargo and VW's problematic decisions most likely were influenced by a combination of failed corporate governance, human cognitive limitations, alliance and coalition influences, a strong desire to maintain [decision] group harmony, and decision process failure closely related to previous minimal decision learning.

Recommendation: Higher-quality decisions are possible, provided ethically-minded managers embrace a management-centered, institutionalized, structured, systematic, objective, and subjective decision process, which Domains of Decision Management purports to provide. Managers who embrace the DDM decision model, incorporate DDM into the organization's culture, and instill the mantra "DDM: Decisions with principles" are destined to achieve more sustainable business practices.

APPENDIX A
Volkswagen (VW) and Wells Fargo (WF) Interviews

The study included a Wells Fargo senior manager together with seven Branch Managers; observations coincided with interviews. Based on the emergent qualitative themes, this researcher concluded the Managers were well versed in their Branch responsibilities and understood organization leadership. Each WF respondent was dedicated to regaining the trust of current and potential customers. All collective case study interviews occurred from February 2019 to August 2019.

VW interviews included five VW Sales Managers, and one VW Repair Shop owner. Observations coincided with the interviews. VW senior management evidence and the company's new business strategy were found on the company website. All respondents were open and candid in their descriptions about how their organizations were regaining and gaining the trust of current and potential VW customers. Interview themes appeared in Table 4. The interview transcripts follow.

Volkswagen Interviews

- **Q5a. What kinds of actions is this dealership doing to regain and gain the trust of current and potential VW customers? VW dealership 1. Respondent VW1.** This Manager began the interview announcing the Jetta diesel now gets 40 miles per gallon. Then he stated, "We at this dealership learned that some, not all customers were upset to be involved in the clean diesel situation." To regain their trust we: 1) have been more customer sensitive and understanding in each case, 2) have displayed sincere honesty in our dealings with customers, and 3) have designated two certified TDI Ambassadors devoting themselves to assisting affected VW owners in hopes of retaining them as VW owners. This Manager began the interview with excitement about the Jetta's new gas mileage. He continued to make clear the dealership's commitment to accommodating customers affected by the scandal. He was open and candid. Positive observations on how this Sales Manager articulated his dealership's response to the VW scandal. [Synopsis: This Sales Manager was laser-focused on making things right for dissatisfied customers, then and now. These behaviors build customer trust.].

- **Q5a. What kinds of actions is this dealership doing to regain and gain the trust of current and potential VW customers? VW dealership 2. Respondent VW2.** This Manager received a lesson in humanity during the height of the clean diesel scandal. He was the dealership's Diesel Ambassador during the scandal period. He, 1) fully embraced the massive lobby banner that states, Customer Satisfaction #1, 2) he embodied sincere friendliness toward customers. To continue, he, 3) stressed honesty and transparency in all dealings, he, 4) made it personal when making things right for the customer, he, 5) sought, and still seeks immediate action concerning dissatisfied customers, and he, 6) received a lesson in humanity while dealing with the best of people and the worst of people. The researcher observed a fully engaged Sales Manager committed to people—[Synopsis: This adaptable Manager was committed to his responsibility of creating satisfied customers. Again, Manager learning and these behaviors build customer trust.].

- **Q5a. What kinds of actions is this dealership doing to regain and gain the trust of current and potential VW customers? VW dealership 3. Respondent VW3.** Regarding the customer: 1) VW credit is available to ease the customer's financing burden. 2) Paramount is taking care of the customer because their automobile issues may vary. 3) This Sales Manager, having three years at the dealership, believed in going above-and-beyond to satisfy customers. [This phrase, stated by the Sales Manager, was original]. 4) Select Sales personnel, when certified as a VW Ambassador, go above-and-beyond to satisfy the customer. 5) The Sales Manager willingly consented to an interview and spoke freely. The customer's first vehicle descriptions are believed. The researcher observed a Sales Manager willing to make decisions benefitting the customer and the dealership. [Synopsis: The Sales Manager welcomed the researcher into the dealership, spoke freely, and was sincerely devoted to satisfying the customers; building customer trust in this dealership appeared to be a top priority.].

- **Q5a. What kinds of actions is this Repair Shop owner doing to regain and gain the trust of current and potential VW customers? VW Shop 4. Respondent VW4.** This repair shop was a small, one-person, specialized business. This VW air- cooled repair shop has been in business for 17 years. VW4: 1) With four VW Beetles, older models, parked outside, he stays busy with jobs. He had 15 engines awaiting his technical skills. He: 2) Was a friendly owner/technician who stated he has 3-6 months of work waiting. Point 3) Quality, to him, meant attention to detail. Last, he not only knows his customers but also knows their vehicles very well. Observation: A small shop, but it was big on technical know-how and personal attention for the customer—[Synopsis: Respondent VW4 was authentic and very committed to his customers. While the location was difficult to find, the interview was enjoyable and was a throwback to the past. His customer commitment builds customer trust.]

- **Q5a. What kinds of actions is this dealership doing to regain and gain the trust of current and potential VW customers? VW dealership 5. Respondent VW5.** 1) Satisfying customers is a dominant mission for this 20-year old dealership. 2) Expert customer service rates first in this organization. 3) The sales staff assembled near the interview discussion, with their collective temperament appeared affable and ready for action. 4) The Sales Manager stated, as a dealership Ambassador, he makes customer contact first to assess his or her needs and desires. He then transfers responsibility to a responsible Service Manager or retains the responsibility if more personal attention is warranted. 5) Corporate social responsibility (CSR) was a big deal in this dealership serving and giving back to its community. The researcher observed an engaged sales staff, and a staff willing to satisfy customers. [Synopsis: What customers remember is not always in-the-dealership service; they may remember how dealership employees gave back to the local community. These service behaviors and CSR involvement build customer trust.]

- **Q5a. What kinds of actions is this dealership doing to regain and gain the trust of current and potential VW customers? VW dealership 6. Respondent VW6.** This Sales Manager was enthusiastic to say: 1) "I love the product." 2) He then bemoaned the fact that today's auto shoppers come fully informed with several offers, placing the dealership at a bargaining disadvantage; it is a buyer's game. VW6 stated, "It is a race to the bottom." Because of this, 3,) providing excellent service is the key; the Service Department adjusts its prices upward, in some cases, to carry the dealership. 4) The clean diesel issue is being addressed head-on; the dealership buys these stored-away vehicles, installs the upgrades, and produces a fully functional and certified VW used automobile. Everyone wins. The in-store TDI Ambassador is the dedicated point person. 5) This Sales Manager was insistent that the dealership participates in community-oriented Corporate Social Responsibility (CSR), such as softball, basketball, food drives, or possibly golf. 6) He spoke, in a very personal way, about his early childhood growing up a few miles from where he now works. He often returns to that neighborhood to inform children about his struggles, in hopes of encouraging them to study and succeed. Observations: This dedicated Service manager was committed to the mission of satisfying customers and giving back to the community—[**Synopsis:** This was a very enlightening interview. Respondent VW6's meager beginnings blossomed into a respected professional who is ready to satisfy customers. Both his leadership and his staff behaviors build customer trust.]

- **Q5b. What kinds of actions is VW senior management doing to regain and gain the trust of current and potential VW customers?** Two email messages sent to VW of America headquarters in Minnesota requesting information as to what the company and senior management were doing to regain the trust of current and potential customers; there were no responses. Undeterred, the researcher visited the VW.com website. Found, was the Volkswagen strategy Together 2025+. This source material found on the company's public website. See Appendix D and read excerpts from the strategy. Included was "Together 4 Integrity," which stated:

> We want Volkswagen to be a company with integrity through and through and to be respected in the best sense of the word.
>
> To meet this requirement, we have created the Group-wide integrity and compliance program Together4Integrity (T4I). It bundles all the activities for

integrity, compliance, culture, risk management, and HR and thus creates the basis for our success.

T4I is our common path towards a corporate culture that enables every manager and every employee to act with integrity and by following the rules at all times and everywhere.

We have summarized our promises to our customers, shareholders, business partners, and ourselves in seven fundamental principles. They describe what the Group stands for in all its brands, companies, and countries:

- We take on responsibility for the environment and society
- We are honest and speak up when something is wrong
- We break new ground
- We live diversity
- We are proud of the work we do.
- WE, not me.
- We keep our word (VW.com, 2019)

Observation: VW appears to have learned from its disastrous diesel scandal. Positive actions are taking shape. A major VW management reorganization is underway to bring new commitment, in an ethical way, to management, customers, and stakeholders.

Wells Fargo Interviews

- **Q6a. What kinds of actions is this Wells Fargo Branch doing to regain and gain the trust of current and potential customers? WF 1. Respondent WF1.** Regarding the customer: 1) place the customer first, 2) listen carefully and be alert, 3) offer the customer all possible product options, and 4) assure the customer that bank security is paramount, requiring two forms of identification in most cases. WF1 stressed to employees: 1) take care of all team members, 2) make sure they have the [bank] knowledge needed to satisfy customers, 3) get the right answers, and 4) communicating with the employees makes a difference. It is a two-way process. This Manager stated the bank's leadership style to Tell-Show-Do-Review. That is, Tell employees the task. If needed, Show them the correct way. Do the job, and Review with the employee. The researcher observed a Manager who was committed to Bank business and employees. [Synopsis: The researcher was impressed; this branch Manager understood bank issues, leadership, and her people. She and her staff were well prepared to continue building customer trust.]

- **Q6a. What kinds of actions is this Wells Fargo Branch doing to regain and gain the trust of current and potential customers? WF 2. Respondent WF2.** Regarding employees, this Manager: 1) expects team members to work together, 2) encourages positive working attitudes, and 3) requires Tellers and Bankers to keep the customer first. He continued by, 4) expecting a positive in-the-bank atmosphere, 5) allowing team members to voice their issues and opinions; they have an open-door policy, and 6) by being a people person. Observations included Bankers coordinating with customers, and the Manager interacting with team members. There were many smiles. The Manager also referred to the bank's leadership style, Tell-Show-Do-Review. This bank was busy. [Synopsis: This Manager directs the activities of a bustling Branch; in so doing, he speaks well and understands leadership, as well as his responsibility to regain customer trust.]

- **Q6a. What kinds of actions is this Wells Fargo Branch doing to regain and gain the trust of current and potential customers? WF 3. Respondent WF3.** Regarding customer support, this Manager: 1) develops and trains employees the correct way. Tellers should: 2) provide the customer with accurate information, 3) follow-up a customer's in-store visit with a phone call, and 4) ask pertinent questions [which, per the literature, demonstrates critical thinking.]. WF3 continued to describe his leadership style: "To be the leader you want to follow." Further, without asking, this Manager felt compelled to describe his leadership style: 1) to teach and develop others, 2) to be passionate, and 3) to be ethical. Observing in this Branch was mainly educational especially the Manager's leadership style. [Synopsis: This Manager voluntarily articulated his leadership style, which was impressive. Together, the Manager and his staff work at being "the leader they want to follow," and as a result, regain customer trust.]

- **Q6a. What kinds of actions is this Wells Fargo Branch doing to regain and gain the trust of current and potential customers? WF 4. Respondent WF4.** The Manager, regarding employees and service to customers: 1) encourage customers to control their finances, 2) state the bank offers the best service possible, 3) recommend customer periodic financial reviews, 4) always be open to addressing customers' concerns, and 5) make a bold effort to participate in corporate social responsibility (CSR). CSR initiatives may be diverse, such as supporting the Big Brother program and donating to different food drives. The researcher observed much enthusiasm toward potential CSR initiatives. This Manager acknowledged the 1/16/2019 Wells Fargo message, *Important Information about the Government Shutdown* that outlined bank products to assist affected customers (Wells Fargo Online, 2019). [Synopsis: The researcher was awed with this Manager's commitment to CSR since these programs give back to the local community. This Manager and the stated employee behaviors build customer trust.]

- **Q6a. What kinds of actions is this Wells Fargo Branch doing to regain and gain the trust of current and potential customers? WF 5. Respondent WF5. WF5.** This Manager encouraged employees to build customer relationships, 1) strive to provide the best customer service, and 2) insist that Bankers and Tellers know their customers [at least on a last-name basis; it is not easy.]. Further, 3) this Manager has planned and candid discussions with employees about significant problems, issues, and opportunities, and 4) this Manager often utilizes the corporate leadership style of Tell-Show-Do-Review (Defined in WF1's interview). This Manager acknowledged the 1/16/2019 Wells Fargo message, *Important Information about the Government Shutdown* that outlined bank products to assist affected customers (Wells Fargo Online, 2019). [Synopsis: Observation: This Manager was a people-oriented leader, which may parallel the finding that "high morale leads to high productivity" (Miles, 1965, 148-155). Remember the wise management-adage, "take care of your people, and they will take care of you." All positive actions to regain customer trust.]

- **Q6a. What kinds of actions is this Wells Fargo Branch doing to regain and gain the trust of current and potential customers? WF 6. Respondent WF6.** This Manager valued quality customer service and community outreach. We, 1) inform the customer we value their business, and 2) demonstrate customer service is a top priority by doing our best. Further, we 3) participate in numerous corporate social responsibility (CSR) initiatives that have a local focus via community outreach, grant programs, and team members volunteering. The Manager acknowledged the 1/16/2019 Wells Fargo message, *Important Information about the Government Shutdown* that outlined bank products to assist affected customers (Wells Fargo Online, 2019). Observation: This branch Manager engendered employee, customer, and CSR interests. [Synopsis: An excellent example of management giving back to the community they love. Customers and people understand this. All positive actions to regain customer trust. Enlightening.]

- **Q6a, What kinds of actions is this Wells Fargo Branch doing to regain and gain the trust of current and potential customers? WF 7. Respondent WF7.** The researcher did not plan this interview; it was an actual customer-manager interaction to an authentic need for financial support. These dealings, actually negotiations, occurred February 2019 in New Mexico. The researcher and his wife were en route to southern Mississippi to comfort a grieving maternal relative. The researcher did not obtain the travel money because of a full work schedule for the previous three days; this made our funding request real. Upon entering a large WF branch, several tellers and the branch Manager were surprising customers stating the bank's nation-wide computer system was down. Deposits Yes, withdrawals No. This lack of funds was potentially a trip-ending roadblock. A lunch break allowed time for system restoration - which did not occur. This researcher sat down with the Branch Manager and explained the need and its sense of urgency. An initial option rejected. Then, the Manager struck pay dirt. A feasible solution was accepted. Money received. The wife, Prince (the thirteen-year-old Cocker Spaniel), and the researcher departed financially satisfied.

Observations: 1) The Manager, in collaboration with the District Manager and Customer Service Manager, provided a valuable service. Additionally, the Manager, 2) was aware of the company's Tell-Show-Do-Review leadership style, and the 1/16/2019 Wells Fargo message, *Important Information about the Government Shutdown* that outlined bank products to assist affected customers (Wells Fargo Online, 2019). The Manager and his staff were observed not only satisfying customers, to the best of their abilities, but also exerting the professional communication and collaboration required to accommodate this researcher in dire need of funds – job well done.

[Synopsis: The researcher's particular financial solution resulted from, 3) a working knowledge of applicable WF policies and procedures and a, 4) well-trained and courteous staff. That day, the researcher personally observed management business activities and Tellers at two different WF locations, 5) being polite and respectful to customers. This Branch Manager and his staff restored this researcher's trust in WF.]

- **Q6b. What kinds of actions is Wells Fargo senior management doing to regain and gain the trust of current and potential customers? WF 8, Respondent WF8.** This WF District Manager received a telephone presentation and interview, from the researcher regarding the collective case study's purpose, origin of documents, DDM theory, and the probing for likely factors contributing to WF questionable decisions. The District Manager listened attentively and questioned on several occasions. The District Manager was informed about the possibility of publishing the study. He also questioned the types of source documents; they were all public-source documents: national and local newspapers, periodicals, recent textbooks, WF Branch Manager interviews and observations.

Following the presentation, the local WF Branch Manager, facilitating the briefing, presented the researcher with two documents: the WF (dated December 31, 2018) Business Standards Report (BSR), 103 pages and a two-page Executive Summary. These documents were invaluable in presenting the Bank in its recovery mode. From these documents, for example, it was learned the Bank had 1) Eliminated product sales goals; 2) Changed incentive, performance management, and recognition programs; 3) Programs are governed by stronger oversight and controls; 5) Reorganized the Board of Directors governance and practices; and 6) Centralized control functions: Corporate Risk, Human Resources, Finance, Technology and Data for increased oversight and consistency. There was much informative content. The study is now in its final stages of completion. The presentation ended with the researcher giving the Bank an 18-page synopsis of the Findings.

These observations were the best, receiving a formal WF statement about their future. Although this was a telephone interview, the District Manager was fully engaged in the researcher's presentation, as well as making available the stated WF BSR info, which indicated he had probably cleared this action with his higher-level managers. [Synopsis: As stated, the WF BSR produced a treasure-trove of information, actions, expected behaviors, and ongoing company actions to reorganize how WF functions.]. See Appendix D.

APPENDIX B
Domains of Decision Management in Action

DDM is a management innovation for the practical purpose of improving managerial decisions. There are three levels of DDM evaluation: formal (F), informal (IF), and single-person (SP). Central to all three are the DDM Terms, Worksheet, Definitions, and instructions. Evaluations: Formal evaluation requires one senior manager, and the Probability Decision Committee (PDC). Other senior managers will support this formal evaluation process. Informal examination is administered by one manager and one knowledgeable supervisor; and SP examination requires one knowledgeable manager or a senior supervisor. DDM examples presented here are Formal and Informal.

2017 Facebook Live Streaming

Recall the Facebook live streaming of the 2017 Cleveland, OH homicide of an innocent man. Facebook's management reaction time was excessively slow, nearly two hours. Live streaming such a horrific event was unprecedented. Subsequently, Facebook managers made several positive decisions; its management announced steps to eliminate the broadcasting of inappropriate and violent material. In addition, 3,000 new hires will be responsible for reviewing videos and other posts to ensure inappropriate materials remain off the site (Associated Press, 2017; Maher, 2017). Justin Osofsky, Facebook's vice president of global operations, acknowledged in a blog post… "That the site's review process is flawed. As a result of this terrible series of events, we are reviewing our reporting flows to be sure people can report videos and other material that violates our standards as easily and quickly as possible" (Steinbuch, 2017). McNamee's (2019) article describes Facebook's true business model:

> The massive success of Facebook eventually led to catastrophe. The business model depends on advertising, which in turn depends on manipulating the attention of users so they see more ads. One best way to manipulate attention is to appeal to outrage and fear, emotions that increase engagement. (p. 24)

Facebook shared 59% of 2017, US digital advertising with Google, is questioning and evaluating improper access and handling of its user data, which resulted in a $36 billion decline in market value (Bercovci, 2018; Tau & Seetharaman, 2018). Because of this, it appears Facebook management decisions are required here also.

DDM exhibits the capability to afford managers a more reactive understanding of pending decisions on internal and external people, time, financials, the organization, and morals and ethics. The caveat, only if managers demonstrate the ability and willingness to do what is ethically right. The DDM operational details follow.

DDM Terms and Worksheet

Table 9a, Domains of Decision Management Formal (F) Worksheet: Facebook Action Required consists mainly of descriptive Fields and Cells that include sensitive qualitative information, quantitative data, and probabilities necessary to examine the potential decision

---

Domains of Decision Management (DDM) Definitions

CD   **Condition Descriptor.** Abbreviated DDM worksheet terms, such as, EthTng, MktCap, OrgPerf, CpttAdv, Repu, Tng, Eval, Empl, CstSat, and others describing circumstances, conditions, behaviors, and other verbiage unique to an organization.

DTARat **Debt-to-Assets Ratio.** Provides information for one point in time. Analysts, investors, and creditors must see subsequent figures to assess a company's progress for reducing its debt (Investopedia, 2019).

CutPri **Current price.** Current price is the most recent selling price of a stock, currency, commodity, or precious metal that is traded on an exchange; the most reliable indicator of that security's present value (Investopedia, 2019).

ED   **Ethical dissonance.** A sense of discomfort or distress that occurs when one's behavior does not correspond to his or her attitudes regarding ethical issues or beliefs (Ciccarelli & White, 2015; Burchard, 2011).

Immediate decisions: **Programmed, routine,** or **re-occurring** decisions, from 2 hours to 24 hours, if not sooner; **Non-programmed, novel,** and **infrequent** decisions, from 24 hours to 48 hours, if not sooner.

JobInv **Job involvement.** The degree, to which a person identifies with a job, actively participates in it, and considers performance important to self-worth (Robbins & Judge, 2015).

JobSat **Job satisfaction.** The collection of feelings and beliefs that managers (and employees) have about their current jobs (Jones & George, 2014).

MktCap **Market capitalization.** The total dollar value of all the company's outstanding shares (Ebert & Griffin, 2015).

MktShe **Market share.** The company's percentage of the total industry sales for a specific product (Ebert & Griffin, 2015).

TSR   **Total shareholder return.** The total amount (i.e., of capital gains and dividends) returned to an investor during a particular time period (Investopedia, 2018).

---

effects to people, time, financials, the organization, and moral and ethical implications – the DDM independent variables.

A description of each field follows:

1. **Problem, Issue, or Opportunity (PIO) (Circle one).** First, decide if the topic of interest is a problem, issue, or an organizational opportunity (PIO). Problems and issues differ in

some respects. A *problem* is a situation that is regarded as unacceptable; an *issue* is a matter about which knowledgeable, informed people disagree to some extent. Solving problems therefore, means *deciding what action will change the situation for the best,* whereas resolving issues means *deciding what belief or viewpoint is the most reasonable* (Ruggiero 2009). *Opportunity* refers to there being a good time or set of circumstances for doing something (Hawker 2006). If multiple options are being compared, indicate this as **"Option 1."** Multiple options require separate DDM Worksheets.

2. **Current topic of interest**. The user develops a concise statement of the PIO formatted as a question. The Table 9a, **Field No. 2**, example is 22 words. Note, in this statement, there are two assertions: first, to evaluate Facebook's streaming service, then, an approximate cause of concern. Be succinct, not wordy.

3. **Evaluation.** Qualitative evaluation of the organization's problem, issue, or opportunity occurs in **Cells 6a to 6e, 7a to 7e**, and **8a to 8e**. Depending on the organization, the condition descriptors in the **DDM Terms and Definitions** may vary, but in many cases, they may not. Users of this tool should adapt and amend the condition descriptor verbiage as required, to be consistent with current company verbiage. Sum the internal and external condition descriptors of vertical Cells 6a + 7a; 6b +7b, 6c + 7c, 6d + 7d, and 6e + 7e. State totals near the bottom of each 7a, b, c, d, and e Cell.

4. **Scoring Alternatives. Field, No. 3**, consists of three quantitative selection alternatives. Score a minus one (-1) or a minus two (-2) for each negative descriptor in **Cells 6a to 7e**. For example, in 6a, Internal, People, there are four descriptors evaluated as minus one (-1) each. In **Cell 7a**, External, People, there are four descriptors evaluated as minus one (-1) each. Total each Domain's condition descriptors; then place

that total as the first number in the Expected Value equation (Mosier, 1989), in **Cells 8a to 8e**. See Table 9a.

Negative two **(-2)** is greater than a negative one **(-1)**, and a positive two **(+2)** is greater than a positive one **(+1)**. Table 9c uses a mixture of negative and positive condition descriptors.

5. **Probability: Probability of Occurrence (PO). Field No. 4,** probability theory has supported decision-makers for years in understanding and selecting many high-dollar projects in which there are elements of uncertainty and risk associated with the alternatives (Honekopp, 2003). Amended slightly for DDM requirements, the expected value for each of the DDM independent variables, is computed as:

> Condition Descriptor total x Probability of Occurrence (PO) = Expected Value (EV)

> **See Field 4.** A percentage is helpful to gauge the **probability of occurrence (PO)** for each set of Domain condition descriptors, both Internal, and External. The DDM Model recommends a maximum decision group of three individuals, Vice Presidents at a minimum, well versed in organizational operations, priorities, and risk management sharing the responsibility of deciding **probability of occurrence (PO).** This expert panel contributes its shared thinking (Maxwell, 2009; Ruggiero, 2009). Larger groups often become stymied in debate, further delaying the decision.

> Determine the PO for each Domain on a scale (.1 to 1.0). Table 9a, **Cells 4a to 4e**, shows an example: People's PO (.8), Time's PO (.7), Financial's PO (.8), the Organization's PO (.8), and Moral and Ethics' PO (.5). These PO quantities are essential in determining the final expected values (EV). Note the vertical totals for **Column 1a, People** equals minus eight (-8). This sum is entered in the 8a equation as:

Condition Descriptor total x Probability of
Occurrence (PO) = Expected Value (EV)

-8 x .8 = -6.4 EV

In a similar way, compute each column's
Expected Value

6. **Determine Action and Expected Values (EV). In Field 5,** are the dispositions of the EVs for each of the five Domains: People, Time, Financials, the Organization, and Morals and Ethics. "The Domain column having, in this case, the greatest negative EV warrants first action." The remaining actions occur in descending numerical order. **A Recommendation for action follows "Here, managers must act to counter internal and externally expected negative impacts, responses, and perceptions."** The five EV equations competing for resources are as indicated below:

1st People EV = -6.4

2nd the Organization EV = -5.6

3rd Financials EV = -4.8

4th Morals and Ethics = -2.5

5th Time EV = -1.4 = -20.7

Collective Total = -20.7

The Collective Total may be compared to other
decision options.

There are "Review for Action" spaces in the lower halves of Cells 8a to 8e.

7. **Multiple decision options require separate DDM Worksheet analysis.**

8. DDM Terms and Definitions

Abst	Absenteeism
CD	Condition Descriptor
ComSup	Community Support
CpttAdv	Competitive Advantage
CSR	Corporate Social Responsibility
Cst	Customer
CstSat	Customer Satisfaction
CulTng	Culture training
CutPri	Current Price
Dec	Decrease
DTARat	Debt-to-Asset Ratio
ED	Ethical dissonance
Empl	Employee
EmplTO	Employee turnover
EthTng	Ethics training
Eval	Evaluation
HR	Human Resources
Inc	Increase
Incong	Incongruence
JobInv	Job Involvement
JobSat	Job satisfaction
LofK	Lack of knowledge
Mgt	Management
MktShe	Market Share
Misund	Misunderstanding
Neg	Negative
Neu	Neutral
OrgPerf	Organization performance
Ovhead	Overhead
PO	Probability of Occurrence
Pos	Positive
Prod	Production
ProdMkt	Production-to-Mkt
Repu	Reputation
Rev	Revenue
Tax	Taxes
Tng	Training
WoM	Word-of-mouth

Table 9a

Domains of Decision Management Formal (F) Worksheet: Facebook Action Required
(One senior manager and the Probability Decision Committee [PDC] complete this worksheet.)

1.(Problem) Issue or Opportunity Option 1 (Circle one)	a. **People**	b. **Time**	c. **Financials**	d. **Organization**	e. **Morals & Ethics**
2. Eval Fields 6a and 7a. The question: What might the impacts be for posting a Cleveland, OH homicide on the company's online streaming service? Mgt reaction time was excessive.	6a.Internal(4) Dec Empl Repu -1 Dec Tust -1 Dec JobSat -1 Inc ED -1	b. Internal (4) Mgt reaction time was excessive -1	c. Internal (4) Dec Rev -1 Dec Profits -1 Dec MktCap -1	d. Internal (4) Dec Org Repu -1 Dec Empl moral -1 Dec Empl JobSat -1 Inc Empl TurnO -1	e. Internal (4) Inc appearance of mgt insensitivity and indifference -1
3. Scoring Alternatives: -1 or -2 for each negative descriptor (A) 0 for each neutral descriptor (B) +1 or +2 for each positive descriptor (C)	7a. External (4) Dec Repu -1 Dec Tust -1 Inc ED -1 CstSat -1 **Total: -8**	b. External (4) Cst reaction time was immediate -1 **Total: -2**	c. External (4) Dec Rev -1 Dec TSR -1 Dec MktCap -1 **Total: -6**	d. External (4) Dec Org Repu -1 Dec Org Tust/Confidence -1 Dec MktShe -1 **Total: -7**	e. External (4) Inc ethical outrage and anger -1 Inc appearance of mrl insensitivity and indifference -1 Inc sharing of action/incident -1 Inc profit motive -1 **Total: -5**
4. Probability of Occurrence (PO) % (.1 to 1.0)	a. PO .8	b. PO .7	c. PO .8	d. PO .8	e. PO .5
5. Expected Value (EV):	8a. EV A. -8 x .8 =(-6.4)	b. EV -2 x .7 = -1.4	c. EV -6 x .8 = -4.8	d. EV -7 x .8 =-5.6	e. EV -5 x .5 = -2.5 (-20.7)
Greatest EV warrants first action.	1st	5th	3rd	2nd	Collective Total 4th
Recommendation: **Immediate mgt decisions required to counter negative effects and perceptions.**	Review for Action:	Review for Action:	Review for Action:	Review for Action:	Review for Action:

Notes:

Table 9b

Domains of Decision Management Formal (F) Worksheet
(One senior manager and the Probability Decision Committee [PDC] complete this worksheet.)

1. Problem, Issue or Opportunity Option 1 (Circle one)	a. People	b. Time	c. Financials	d.Org	e. M & E
2. Eval Fields 6a and 7a. The question:	6a Internal (4)	b. Internal (4)	c. Internal (4)	d. Internal (4)	e. Internal (4)
3. Scoring Alternatives: -1 or -2 + Neg (A) 0 = Neu (B) +1 or +2 = Pos (C)	7a External (4)	b. External (4)	c. External (4)	d. External (4)	e. External (4)
	Total:	Total:	Total:	Total:	Total:
4. Probability of Occurrence (PO) % (.1 to 1.0) PO →	a. PO	b. PO	c. PO	d. PO	e. PO
5. Expected Value (EV): →	8a. Totals ◯	b. Totals	c. Totals	d. Totals	e. Totals ◯
Greatest EV warrants first action					
Recommendation:					Collective Total

Notes:

Table 9c
Domains of Decision Management Informal (IF) Worksheet: Example
(One manager, one knowledgeable supervisor, and the Probability Decision Committee [PDC] complete this worksheet)

1. Opportunity Option 1	a. People	b. Time	c. Fin	d. Org	e. M&E
2. ? What effect(s) will new Prod site have? Expectations positive.	6a. Int (4) Empl +1 Inc Prod +1 Dec Empl TO +1 Inc Job Inv +1	b. Int (4) Dec Prod +1 Dec ProdMkt +1	c. Int (4) Inc HR -2 Inc Rev +1 Dec DTARat +1 Inc Tax -2	d. Int (4) Inc MktShe +1 Inc MktCap +1 Inc Repu +1 Inc Ovhd -1	e. Int (4) CulTng +1 EthTng +1
3. Scoring -1 or -2 = Neg 0=Neu +1 or +2 = Pos	7a. Ext (4) CSR +1 Inc Repu +1 PosWoM +1 **Total: 7**	b. Ext (4) Inc CstSat +1 **Total: 3**	c. Ext (4) Inc TSR +1 Inc Rev +1 **Total:0**	d. Ext (4) Inc CstSat +1 Inc Repu +1 Inc OrgPerf +1 Pos CpttAdv +1 **Total: 6**	e. Ext (4) Inc ComSup +1 **Total: 3**
4. Probability of Occurrence (%) (.1 to 1.0)	a. PO .7	b. PO .8	c. PO .7	d. PO .7	e. PO .8
5. Expected Value (EV)	EV 7x.7 = 4.9	EV 3x.8 = 2.4	EV 0x.7 = 0	EV 6x.7 = 4.2	EV 3x.8= 2.4
First action to Greatest EV	1	3, 4	5	2	3, 4
Recommend: Approve site.					Collective Total +13.9

APPENDIX C
Critical Thinking: Asking Questions

According to Browne and Keeley (2015), "Critical thinking begins with the desire to improve what we think" (p. 4). This may apply to numerous situations, problems, issues, or business opportunities. As argued, the subject companies needed an ethical focus to treat customers fairly and to treat all stakeholders the way the decision-makers desired to be treated – the *Golden Rule*. These authors advise to slow down when considering things.

Table 10
Critical Thinking: Asking Questions

- What are the internal and external effects on people?
- What are the internal and external effects on time?
- What are the internal and external effects on financials?
- What are the internal and external effects on the organization?
- What are the internal and external moral and ethical implications?
- What is the problem, issue, or opportunity and the conclusion?
- What are the reasons?
- Are there ambiguous words or phrases?
- Are the assumptions known?
- Are there any fallacies in the reasoning?
- Question the statistics?
- Question the evidence: personal experience, personal observation, research studies, testimonials, and appeals to authority?
- Are there rival factors?
- Is noteworthy information omitted?
- What realistic conclusions are possible?

Critical thinking is both an art and a science. It is Art because there is beauty in one's quest for knowledge. It is, to some extent, a Science, because of the systematic study and processes needed to ask and obtain quality, timely, complete, and relevant responses to the critical questions above. Science introduces rigor and thoroughness to ferret out the details.

APPENDIX D
Wells Fargo and Volkswagen's New Business Strategies

Q6b. CCS. What kinds of actions is Wells Fargo senior management doing to regain and gain the trust of current and potential customers?

An Apology
[This title is the researcher's interpretation]

WF has a long history of serving customers through trusted relationships and products and services that help customers succeed financially. We clearly broke that trust through unacceptable sales practices in our Community Bank and issues in other businesses. Our actions resulted in customer harm and caused significant damage to our reputation. We are sorry, and are working hard to make things right.

(WF *Business Standards Report*, 2018)

Steps to Regain Trust

- Eliminated product sales goals;
- Changed incentive, performance management, and recognition programs;
- Programs are governed by stronger oversight and controls;
- Reorganized the Board of Directors governance and practices; and
- Centralized control functions: Corporate Risk, Human Resources, Finance, Technology, and Data for increased oversight and consistency

(WF *Business Standards Report*, 2018)

Team Members and Customers

WF has learned from its past; we have put into practice: Increased transparency and engagement with team members, customers, and other stakeholders. Via meetings with team members, surveys, and other means, productive actions have been taken for team members:

- Holding all-team town hall meetings with the CEO by monthly
- Simplifying our Vision, Values, & Goals focusing on what is important
- Enhancing our allegations process to address concerns about retaliation
- Increasing team member training and development, raising the US minimum base pay, adding more paid holidays, and granting restricted stock awards to about 250,000 team members
- We now seek input on our culture and ways to improve it

For customers:

- We are committed to providing remediation to customers who were harmed by unacceptable retail banking practices and issues in other businesses and making things right.
- We are also focused on improving the customer experience . . . by offering new and more convenient ways to do business with us, and enhancing important functions such as monitoring, reporting, and escalating customer complaints
- We remain focused on delivering on our vision to satisfy their financial needs and help them succeed financially   (WF *Business Standards Report*, 2018)

Q5. CCS. What kinds of actions is VW senior management doing to regain and gain the trust of current and potential VW customers?

Together 4 Integrity

We want Volkswagen to be a company with integrity through and through and to be respected in the best sense of the word.

To meet this requirement, we have created the Group-wide integrity and compliance program Together4Integrity (T4I). It bundles all the activities for integrity, compliance, culture, risk management, and HR and thus creates the basis for our success. T4I is our common path towards a corporate culture that enables every manager and every employee to act with integrity and in accordance with the rules at all times and everywhere.

We have summarized our promises to our customers, shareholders, business partners, and ourselves in seven key principles. They describe what the Group stands for in all its brands, companies, and countries:

- We take on responsibility for the environment and society
- We are honest and speak up when something is wrong
- We break new ground
- We live diversity
- We are proud of the work we do.
- WE not me
- We keep our word   (VW.com, 2019)

Best Governance: Focused, Lean, Trustworthy

The Volkswagen Group has already taken important steps to streamline its structures and make decision-making processes more decentralized. But we still have potential - and want to constantly improve. In the "Best Governance" module, we address deficits in a structured and consistent manner: We streamline our committees, reduce bureaucracy, and streamline Group administration considerably. We are systematically checking whether we are still the best owner for the various divisions. We are using a decarburization index to make our CO2 targets measurable and our progress transparent. And we are intensifying the dialogue with all key stakeholders in order to regain and further build trust.

Our goal: We form a focused, lean Group holding company that optimally manages its brands and continuously leverages synergies within the Group. Our stakeholders perceive Volkswagen as an efficiently managed, trustworthy, sustainable, and transparent Group. As a company that creates value in every aspect and powerfully shapes mobility for us – and for future generations.   (VW.com, 2019)

Shaping Mobility—for Generations to Come

Volkswagen has always made individual and affordable mobility possible for millions of people. Under the new vision, . . . we are providing answers to the challenges of today and tomorrow with our sharpened TOGETHER 2025+ Group strategy. Our goal is to make mobility sustainable for us and for future generations. Our promise: With electric drive, digital networking and autonomous driving, we make the automobile clean, quiet, intelligent and safe. At the same time, our core product becomes even more emotional and offers a completely new driving experience. It is also becoming part of the solution when it comes to climate and environmental protection. In this way, the car can continue to be a cornerstone of contemporary, individual, and affordable mobility in the future.
                                    (VW.com, 2019)

Excellent Leadership: Versatile, Integrity, Strong Leader

In order to be successful in the new world of mobility, we must make rapid progress towards an open, cooperative, and integrated management culture.

In the "Excellent Leadership" module, we are creating the prerequisites for this: We are fundamentally restructuring our management development and qualifications. We systematize succession planning in order to have the right talents in the right positions at the right time. We want to increase significantly the diversity of our management team. That is why we are setting ourselves clear, measurable goals for more female and international managers.

The common goal: By 2025, Volkswagen will set an example for others with open, partnership-based, value-based leadership. Our management development sets standards. We live and reward entrepreneurship and future-oriented thinking every day. We live diversity at all levels.   (VW.com, 2019)

K-I Integrity and Legal Affairs

The trust our customers continue to place in us and the perception of Volkswagen as an excellent employer are crucial for the Group's success. The strategic objective of the Integrity and Legal Affairs functional area is therefore to anchor these factors as the basis for daily activities in the Group, thereby making a vital contribution to Volkswagen's sustainable growth. This specifically entails safeguarding customers and staff against compliance risks and positioning the functional area as a competence center for integrity and legal affairs, data protection, compliance and risk management.

(VW.com, 2019)

References

Abdellah, I. M. (2016). A grounded theory study of decision making within informal work environments. Electronic dissertation. *University of Liverpool.* http://ethos.bl.uk/OrderDetails.do?uin=uk.bl.ethos.733799

Amar, M., Ariely, D., Carmon, Z., & Yang, H. (2018, April). How counterfeits infect genuine products: The role of moral disgust. *Journal of Consumer Psychology, 28*(2), 329-343.

Argyris, C. (1991, May-June). Teaching smart people how to learn [Single loop and double loop learning and decision making]. *Harvard Business Review, 69*(3), 99-109.

Associated Press. (2017, May 4). Facebook ramps up its response to violent videos. *Sierra Vista Herald*, p. A8.

AT&T. (2019). Changing the path for diversity and inclusion. *Fortune, 178*(1), 16.

Bach, D. (2015, September 26). Seven reasons Volkswagen is worse than Enron. *FT Confidential Research.* https://www.ft.com/cms/s/0/cf9f73e8-62d6-11e5-9846-de406ccb37f2.html#axzz-41V16gCCh

Back, A. (2016, September 10-11).Well's questionable Cross-Sales. *The Wall Street Journal*, p. B12.

Bahler, K. (2019, January - February). My trick to beating anxiety at work. *Money, 48*(1), 22.

Bansal, T., King, M., & Seijts, G. (2015, September 26; Updated 2018, May 15). The Volkswagen emissions scandal: A case study in corporate misbehavior. *The Globe and Mail.* https://www.the-globeandmail.com/

Basu, K. (2014). The Ponzi economy. *Scientific American, 310*(6), 70-75. https://doi.org/10.1038/scientificamerican0614-70

Bell, L. R., Raiffa, H., & Tversky, A. (Eds.). (1988). *Decision making: Descriptive, normative, and prescriptive interactions.* Cambridge University Press.

Bercovci, J. (2018, May). The problem with the platforms: Giant tech companies love founders. Until they start getting too successful. *Inc.*, 11-12.

Berger, P. L., & Luckmann, T. (1967). *The social construction of reality: A treatise in the sociology of knowledge* [It may readily be conceded that contemporary Western men, largely, live in a world vastly different from any preceding one (p. 188)]. Anchor.

Bernard, H. R., & Ryan, G. W. (2010). *Analyzing qualitative data* [For a very brief introduction to the method]. Sage.

Birkinshaw, J., Hamel, G., & Mol, M. J. (2008). Management innovation. *Academy of Management Review, 33*(4), 825-845. https://doi.org/10.4236/ajibm.2016.61005

Blanchard, K., & Johnson, S. (1982). *The one minute manager* [Excellent leadership techniques]. Berkley Books.

Boddy, C. R. (2011, Spring). The corporate psychopaths theory of global financial crisis. *Journal of Business Ethics*, 102, 256.

Boehmer, K. S. (Ed.). (2001). *American Heritage dictionary of idioms.* Houghton Mifflin.

Bomey, N. (2018, June 19). Audi CEO Stadler arrested in emissions scandal fallout. *USA Today*, p. 4B.

Boston, W. (2018, April 11). Volkswagen prepares to replace CEO. *The Wall Street Journal*, pp. B1, B2.

Boston, W., & Norman, L. (2019, April 6-7). BMW to take $1 billion charge for antitrust fine. *The Wall Street Journal*, p. B3.

Botti, S., & Cloney, E. (2016). Being choosey about choice. *London Business School Review, 27*(2), 10-13. https://doi.org/10.1111/2057-1615.12109/abstract

Brooks, L. J., & Dunn, P. (2018). *Business & professional ethics for directors, executives, & Accountants* (7th ed.). Cengage Learning.

Browne, M. N., & Keeley, S. M. (2015). *Asking the right questions: A guide to critical thinking* (11th ed.). Pearson.

Burchard, M. J. (2011). Ethical dissonance and response to destructive leadership: A proposed model. *Emerging Leadership Journal, 4*(1), 154-176.

Bush, M. C., & Lewis-Kulin, S. (2017). *Fortune's* 100 best companies to work for. *Fortune, 175*(4), 79-139.

Bush, M. C., & Tkczyk, C. (2019). *Fortune's* 100 best companies to work for. *Fortune, 179*(3), 57-80.

Calabresi, M. (2016, October 3). Wells Fargo customer fraud deals political setback to banks. *Time, 188*(13), 14.

Calfas, J. (2020, March 13). In US, [COVID-19] threat upends daily life. *The Wall Street Journal*, pp. A1, A6.

Cameron, K. S., & Quinn, R. E. (2011). *Diagnosing and changing organizational culture*. Jossey-Bass.

Carmody, T. (2011, May). How giving 110% is actually possible. *KOTTKE.ORG*. https://kottke.org/11/05/how-giving-110-is-actually-possible.

Carucci, R. (2016). *Early lessons from Wells Fargo: Three ways to prevent ethical failure. Forbes*. https://www.forbes.com/sites/roncarucci/2016/09/13/early-lessons-from-wells-fargo-3-ways-to-prevent-ethical failure/#4318372d6a9

Chevron Corporation. (2018). *Chevron: 2017 annual report: Corporate responsibility highlights*. https://www.chevron.com

Chew, J., Griffith, E., Hackett, R., Kowitt, B., Lev-Ram, M., Lorenzetti, L., Marinova, P., Primack, D., & Rao, L. (2016). The *Fortune* Entrepreneurs. *Fortune, 173*(3), 98-106.

Ciccarelli, S. K., & White, J. N. (2015). *Psychology* (4th ed.). Pearson.

Clozel, L., & Ackerman, A. (2019, February 19). Wells Fargo Chief to face panel alone. *The Wall Street Journal*, p. B6.

Cohen, M. D., March, J. G., & Olsen, J. P. (1972). A garbage-can model of organizational choice. *Administrative Science Quarterly, 17*, 1-25.

Colias, M. (2018, November 27). GM to close plants, cut jobs. *The Wall Street Journal*, pp. A1, A8.

Collins, J. (2001). *Good to great: Why some companies make the leap . . . and others don't.* [Demonstrated leadership qualities]. HarperBusiness.

Colvin, G. (2019). AT&T's heavy lift. *Fortune, 179*(6), 102-110.

Cooper, D. R., & Schindler, P. S. (2011). *Business research methods* (11th ed.) [Excellent treatment of Limitations]. McGraw-Hill Irwin.

Cowley, S. (2016, November 4). Scrutiny for Wells Fargo over ex-employee files. *The New York Times,* pp. B1, B6.

Cowley, S., & Flitter, E. (2018, December 28). Wells Fargo agrees to pay $575 million to resolve state investigations. *The New York Times* (National ed.). https://www.nytimes.com

Creswell, J. W. (2013). *Qualitative inquiry and research design: Choosing among five approaches* (3rd ed.). Sage.

Creswell, J. W. (2014). *Research design: Qualitative, quantitative, and mixed methods approaches* (4th ed.). Sage.

Current price, Debt-to-asset, Total shareholder return. (2018, 2019). *Investopedia.* https://www.investopedia.com/terms

Cyert, R. M., & March, J. G. (1963, 1992). *A behavioral theory of the firm.* Prentice-Hall. Blackwell.

Daft, R. L. (2016). *Organization theory & design* (12th ed.). Cengage Learning.

DeCarlo, S., & Rapp, N. (2016). The Global 500 matrix; The list; Notes and Index. *Fortune, 174*(2), 110, F-1, F-7.

Dessler, G. (2001). *Management: Leading people and organizations in the 21st century.* Prentice Hall.

Dessler, G. (2018). *Fundamentals of human resource management* (4th ed.). Pearson India Education.

Dhami, M. K., & Thomson, M. E. (2012). On the relevance of Cognitive Continuum Theory a Quasirationality for understanding management judgment and decision making. *European Management Journal, 30,* 316-326. https://doi.org/10.1016/j.emj.2012.02.002

Drucker, P. F. (1966). *The effective executive* [Excellent treatment of the rational decision-making process for managers, which is teachable]. HarperBusiness.

Drucker, P. F. (2001). *The essential Drucker: The best of sixty years of Peter Drucker's essential writings on management.* Collins Business.

Ebert, R. J., & Griffin, R. W. (2015). *Business essentials* (10th ed.). Pearson.

Eddy, M. (2019, July 31). Rupert Stadler, Ex-Audi Chief, is charged with fraud in diesel scandal. *The New York Times.* https://www.nytimes.com/2019/07/31/business/audi-diesel-emissions-rupert-stadler.html

Edmondson, A. C. (2012). *Teaming: How organizations learn, innovate, and compete in the knowledge economy.* Jossey-Bass.

Egan, M. (2016). 5,300 Wells Fargo employees fired over 2 million phony accounts. *CNN Money.* https://money.cnn.com/2016/09/08/investing/wells-fargo-created-phony-accounts-bank-fees/index.html

Eisen, B. (2020, February 22-23). Wells Fargo [WF] settles US probes [L.A. prosecutors said the sell practices date to 1998, when sales growth became a priority]. *The Wall Street Journal,* pp. A1, A10.

Ensign, R. L. (2019, December 5). Wells Fargo's list of woes grows. *The Wall Street Journal.* pp. A1, A8.

Ensign, R. L., & Kellaher, C. (2019, November 15). Wells Fargo legal chief to depart. [First published in *The Wall Street Journal,* (Date above). Republished (2019, November 15) by *Dow Jones Newswires*], https://eresearch.fidelity.com/eresearch/evaluate/news/basicNewsStory.jhtml?symbols=WFC%2FPP&story-id=201911150247DOWJONESDJONLINE000144&sb=1

Elson, R. J., & Ingram, P. (2018). Wells Fargo and the unauthorized customer accounts: A case study. *Global Journal of Business Pedagogy, 2*(1), 124-134.

Ewing, J. (2017a, February 2). So, VW has settled. What does it mean for vehicle owners? *The New York Times,* p. B5.

Ewing, J. (2017b, February 2). Bosch will pay millions for role in VW scandal. *The New York Times,* pp. B1, B5.

Ewing, J. (2018, April 19). Porsche Board member among targets as [German] Police raid offices in emissions scandal. *The New York Times,* p. B2.

Ewing, J. (2019, September 24). VW Executives and Ex-CEO are charged with Market manipulation [VW acknowledged its company culture was toxic. A senior VW executive has been working to change the company's authoritarian culture.]. *The New York Times.* https://www.nytimes.com/2019/09/24/business/volkswagen-executives-market-manipulation.html?action=click&module=Well&pgtype=Homepage&section=Business

Ewing, J., & Mouawad, J. (2015, October 23). Directors say Volkswagen delayed informing them of trickery. *The New York Times.* https://www.nytimes.com/2015/10/24/business/international/directors-say-volkswagen-delayed-informing-them-of   -trickery.html

Ferrell, O. C., Fraedrich, J., & Ferrell, L. (2019). *Business ethics: Ethical decision making and cases* (12th ed.). Cengage Learning.

Festinger, L. (1957). *A theory of cognitive dissonance.* Stanford University Press.

Fischer, H. (2018, May 2). Volkswagen settles Ariz. Fraud charges for $40M. *Arizona Daily Star*, pp. A1, A4.

Flitter, E., Appelbaum, B., & Enrich, D. (2018, February 4). How Wells Fargo [WF] and Federal Reserve struck deal to hold Bank's board accountable [An unprecedented action that forced WF to reorganize its Board]. *The New York Times.* https://www.nytimes.com

Flitter, E., Cowley, S., & Enrich, D. (2019, March 29). Wells Fargo loses Chief amid tumult. *The New York Times*, pp. B1, B3.

Fortune.com. (2018). The annual *Fortune* 500. *Fortune, 177*(6), F1-F48.

Fortune Global 500. (2006-2019). The *Fortune* Global 500. https://fortune.com/global500/2016/search/

Gamble, J. E., Peteraf, M. A., & Thompson, A. A. (2017). *Essentials of strategic management: The quest for competitive advantage* [Sustainable business practices beget many positive outcomes]. (5th ed.). McGraw-Hill Education.

Gates, G., Keller, J., Russell, K., & Watkins, D. (2015, October 2). How Volkswagen got away with diesel deception. *The New York Times.* https:// www.nytimes.com

Glazer, E. (2016a, September, 17-18). Wells Fargo [WF] tripped by its culture: Hourly targets and fear of firings drove employees to break rules [Banking rivals attempted to emulate WF sells successes]. *The Wall Street Journal*, pp. A1, A8.

Glazer, E. (2016b, September, 17-18). On the way to great; Six products per customer [Perhaps our new cheer should be "Let's go again for ten"]. *The Wall Street Journal*, p. A8.

Glazer, E. (2017a, March 10). Wells Fargo shakes up retail unit. *The Wall Street Journal*, p. B9.

Glazer, E. (2017b, September 1). Wells Fargo raises its tally of fake accounts. *The Wall Street Journal*, pp. A1, A8.

Glazer, E. (2017c, April 11). Wells Slams former bosses' high-pressure sales tactics. *The Wall Street Journal*, pp. A1, A9.

Glazer, E. (2018, December 6). Wells [Fargo] fires area chiefs over sales scandal. *The Wall Street Journal*, pp. B1, B8.

Gleeson, S. (2020, March 13). No March Madness 'devastating' for players. *USA Today*, p. 2C.

Goldstein, D. (2017, August 11). In High School, the workplace comes first. *The New York Times*, pp. A1, A14.

Guba, E. G. (1990). *The alternative paradigm dialog.* In E. G. Guba (Ed.). *The paradigm dialog* (pp. 17-30). Sage.

Hakim, D., Kessler, A. M., & Ewing, J. (2015, September 26). As VW pushed to be No. 1, ambitions fueled a scandal. *The New York Times.* https://www.nytimes/2015/09/27/business/as-vw-pushed-to-be-no-1-ambitions-fueled-a-scandal.htmp

Hammond, K. R. (2010). Intuition No!…Quasirationality, Yes. *Psychological Inquiry, 21*(4), 327-337. https://doi.org/10.1080/1047 840X.2010.521483

Hatch, M. J., & Cunliffe, A. L. (2013). *Organization theory: Modern, symbolic, and postmodern perspectives* (3rd ed.). Oxford University Press.

Hawker, S. (Ed.). (2006). *Oxford English dictionary* (3rd ed.). Oxford University Press.

Heid, M. (2019). *Are some of us wired to achieve?* In E. Felsenthal, (Ed.). *The science of success. Time,* Meredith Corporation.

Heimer, M., & DeCarlo, S. (2020). The world's most admired companies, *Fortune, 181*(2), 121-123.

Higgins, J. (1994). *101 creative problem solving techniques: The handbook of new ideas for business.* New Management Publishing.

Hirsch, E. D., Kett, J. F., & Trefil, J. (2002). *The new dictionary of cultural literacy* (3rd ed.). Houghton Mifflin Company.

Hofweber, T. (2013, Spring). "Logic and Ontology," In *The Stanford Encyclopedia of Philosophy*, E. N. Zalta, (Ed.). http://plato.stanford.edu/archives/spr2013/entries/logic-ontology/

Honekopp, J. (2003). Precision of probability information and prominence of outcomes: A description and evaluation of decisions under uncertainty. *Organizational Behavior and Human Decision Processes, 90,* 124. https://doi.org/10.2307/1423035

Husserl, E. (2000). *Logical investigations* [Phenomenological suspending of judgement and biases]. (Vols. 1-2). Humanity Books.

Janis, I. L. (1982). *Groupthink: Psychological studies of policy decisions and fiascoes* [Groupthink causes questionable quality decisions]. (2nd ed.). Houghton-Miffin.

Johnson, K., & McCoy, K. (2016, September 15). Federal prosecutors probe Wells Fargo. *USA Today*, p. 2B.

Jones, G. R., & George, J. M. (2014). *Essentials of contemporary management* (8th ed.). McGraw-Hill.

Jonsen, A. R., & Toulmin, S. (1998). *The abuse of casuistry.* University of California Press.

Kant, I. (1788). *Critique of practical reason* [Statement of Kant's categorical imperative – the *Golden Rule*]. (Translated by T. K. Abbott). Encyclopaedia Britannica, Inc.

Keeny, R. L., & Raiffa, H. (1976). *Decisions with multiple objectives: Preferences and value tradeoffs.* John Wiley & Sons. https://doi.org/10.1109/TSMC.1979.4310245

Kida, A. T., Moreno, K. K., & Smith, J. F. (2010). Investment decision making: Do experienced decision makers fall prey to the Paradox of Choice? *Journal of Behavioral Finance, 11*(1), 21-30.

Kohlberg, L. (1969). *Stage and Sequence: The cognitive developmental approach to Socialization* [A maturity process regarding one's moral development]. In *Handbook of socialization and theory and research*, D. A. Goslin (Ed). Rand McNally.

Kouzes, K. M., & Posner, B. Z. (2003). *Credibility: How leaders gain and lose it, why people demand it* [Demonstrated leadership qualities]. Jossey-Bass.

Krantz, M. (2016, October 13). Wells Fargo CEO abruptly departs. *USA Today*, p. 1A.

Kuhn, T. S. (1970). *The structure of scientific revolutions*, Rev. (2nd ed.). University of Chicago Press.

Lashinsky, A. (2019). Hot under the white collar. *Fortune, 179*(1), 7-9.

Lashinsky, A. (2020). The conversation: Sundar Pichai [The new CEO of Google and parent Alphabet]. *Fortune, 181*(2), 14-18.

Leedy, P. D., & Ormrod, J. E. (2019). *Practical research: Planning and design* (12th ed.). Pearson.

Levering, R., Bartulski, E., Chew, J., Frauenheim, E., Groden, C., Moskowitz, M., & Russell, T. (2016). *Fortune's* 100 best companies to work for. *Fortune, 173*(4), 141-165.

Levitt, H., & Dexheimer, E. (2020, March 10). Wells Fargo CEO tells lawmakers bank has 'Sense of Urgency.' *Bloomberg* LP, https:www.bloomberg.com/news/articles/2020-03-10/wells-fargo-ceo-tells-lawmakers-bank-has-new-sense-of-urgency

Likert, R. (1961). *New patterns of management*. McGraw-Hill.

Lincoln, Y. S., & Guba, E. G. (1985). *Naturalistic Inquiry.* Sage.

Lockie, A. (2015, May 14). "Nestlé Waters' CEO will 'Absolutely Not' stop bottling water in California – In fact, I could I'd increase it." *Business Insider.*

Lynch, E. (2020, March 13). Uncertain Spring surrounds Players [Golf Tournament]. *USA Today*, pp. 1- 2C.

Macklin, R., & Mathison, K. (2018). Embedding ethics: Dialogic partnerships and communitarian business ethics. *Journal of Business Ethics, 153*(1), 133-145. https://doi.org/10.1007/s10551-016-3431-0

Macrotrends LLC. (2020, April 6). Wells Fargo revenue 2006-2019. *Macrotrends.net*. [Fundamental data from Zacks Investment Research, Inc.]. https://www.macrotrends.net/stocks/charts/WFC/wells-fargo/revenue

Maglich, J. (2013). Madoff ponzi scheme, five years later. *Forbes.*

http://www.Forbes.com/sites/jordenmaglich/2013/12/09/Mad-off-ponzi-scheme-fiveslater/#3c7766ac789f

Maher, K. (2017, April 19). Suspected killer shoots self dead after car chase. *The Wall Street Journal*, p. A3.

Mahler, A. (2015). VW sandal: Time for German industry to abandon its arrogance. *Spiegel Online International*. https://www.spiegal.de/international/business/vw-scandal-shows-german-companies-are-no-longer-big-league-a-1055098.html

March, J., & Simon, H. A. (1958). *Organizations* (2nd ed.) [An influential work addressing organization communications and the institutionalization of innovation]. Blackwell.

Marya, R. (2019). The best workplaces for diversity. *Fortune, 178*(1), 18.

Mashayekhi, R. (2020). *Fortune's* 100 best companies to work for. *Fortune, 181*(3), 115-120.

Mason, R. O. (1969). A dialectic approach to strategic planning. *Management Science*, 13, 403-414.

Mathews, S., & Smith, G. B. (Eds.). (2015). *Dictionary of religion and ethics*. Forgotten Books.

Maxwell, J. C. (2003). *Thinking for a change: 11 ways highly successful people approach life and work*. Hachette Book Group.

Maxwell, J. C. (2009). *How successful people think: Change your thinking, change your life*. Center Street.

Mayer, J. D., & Salovey, P. (1997). *What is emotional intelligence?* In P. Salovey & D. Sluyter (Eds.), *Emotional development, and emotional intelligence: Educational implications* (pp. 3-31). Basic Books.

McGee, P. (2019a, May 5). VW profit falls less than expected in tough quarter for carmakers: Revenue edge higher to €60 billion despite drag from diesel scandal and lower unit sales. *The Financial Times*. https://www.ft.com/content/6360ab20-6caa-11e9-a9a5-351eeaef6d84?desktop=true&segmentId=7c8f09b9-9b61-4fbb-9430-9208a9e233c8#myft:notification:daily-email:content

McGee, P. (2019b, May 7). Porsche fined €535 million by German prosecutors over diesel scandal. *The Financial Times*. https://www.ft.com

McGee, P., & Storbeck, O. (2019, April 15). German prosecutors charge former Volkswagen CEO with fraud [This paper reports the clean-diesel deception occurred 2006 to 2015.]. *The Financial Times*. https://www.ft.com/content/06ed4398-5f77-11e9-b285-3acd5d43599e

McKinsey & Company. (2009, January). How companies make good decisions: McKinsey Global Survey Results. *The McKinsey Quarterly*. https://www.mckinseyquarterly.com

McNamee, R. (2019, January). How to fix social media before it's too late: An early investor on how Facebook lost its way. *Time, 193*(3), 22-28.

McWhirter, C. (2019, July 15). [Hurricane] Barry mostly spares metro New Orleans. *The Wall Street Journal*, p. A3.

Michaelson, C. (2018). A novel approach to business ethics education: Exploring how to live and work in the 21st century. *Academy of Management Learning & Education, 15*(3), 588-606.

Miles, R. E. (1965, July-August). Human relations or human resources. *Harvard Business Review, 43*(4), 148-155.

Mills, G. E. (2018). *Action research: A guide for the teacher researcher* (6th ed.). Pearson.

Moffett, J. E. (1988, July-August). DOD's [US Department of Defense] live-in employees. *The Manager*, 7(4), 12. [A Boeing Company publication].

Moffett, J. E., Sr. (2017). *Certificate of Registration: Domains of decision management: A treatise in the methodology of managerial decision making* [Unpublished theory paper]. [Claimant: James E. Moffett, Sr., Registration number: Txu-2-041-986, Effective date of registration: July 25, 2017]. US Copyright Office.

Mosier, R. C. (1989, July). Expected value: Applying research to uncertainty. *Appraisal Journal*, 289-296.

Moss, T. (2020, February 18). Some VW plants stay closed. *The Wall Street Journal*, p. B2.

Moustakas, C. (1994*). Phenomenological research methods* [Suspending preconceived notions, biases, and judgements is termed *Epoche*, (pp. 22, 26)]. Sage.

Nachtwey, J. (2018, March). The opioid diaries [Untold opioid struggles are heartbreaking]. *Time, 191*(9), 12-60.

Neal, L., & Spetzler, C. (2015, December 6). Best decisions involve whole company. *Harvard Business Review*. In *Boston Globe*. https://search.proquest.com/docview/1739353288?accountid=458

Nelson, D. L., & Cooper, C. L. (2007). *Positive organizational behavior*. Sage.

Nieves, J. (2016). Outcomes of Management innovation: An empirical analysis in the Services industry. *European Management Review, 13*(2), 125-136. https://doi.org/10.1111/emre.12071

Nor, R. A., Hollenbeck, J. R., Gerhart, B., & Wright, P. M. (2019). *Human resource management: Gaining a competitive advantage* (11th ed.). McGraw Hill Education.

Pearce, J. A. II, & Robinson, R. B. (2013). *Strategic management: Planning for domestic & global competition* (13th ed.). McGraw-Hill Irwin.

Perrow, C. (1961, December). Goals in complex organizations. *American Sociological Review, 26*(6), 854-865.

Perrow, C. (2014). *Complex organizations: A critical essay*. Echo Point Books & Media.

Peters, T. J., & Waterman, R. H. Jr. (1982). *In search of excellence: Lessons from America's best-run companies*. Warner Books.

Pfeffer, J. (1981). *Power in Organizations*, XI, 337. Pitman Publishing.

Pfeffer, J., & Salancik, G. R. (2003). *The external control of organizations: A resource dependent perspective* [Information that is questioned, researched and retained, especially from external sources, is likely to emphatically shape decisions (p. 13)]. Stanford University Press.

Pfeffer, J., & Sutton, R. I. (2006). Evidence-based management. *Harvard Business Review, 84*(1), 62-74.

Porter, M. E. (1985). *Competitive advantage: Creating and sustaining superior performance*. The Free Press.

Quinn, R. E. (1988). *Beyond rational management: Mastering the paradoxes and competing demands of high performance*. Jossey-Bass.

Quinn, E. (2018). Allan Stanford Ponzi scheme. *Investment.com*. https://www.investmentzen.com/news/10-worst-cases-of-corporate-greed-in-us-history/

Ragin, C. C. (2014). *The comparative method: Moving beyond qual-*

itative and quantitative strategies. University of California Press. [Original work published in 1987].

Ragin, C. C., & Becker, H. S. (1992). *What is a case? Exploring the foundations of social inquiry.* Cambridge University Press.

Ragin, C. C., & Amoroso, L. M. (2011). *Constructing social research* [For a slightly longer but very accessible introduction to the method by its originator, C. C. Ragin]. (2nd ed.). Sage.

Reuters. (2019, December 20). Volkswagen takes one-two punch in Australia with fine, Lawsuit. *The New York Times.* Contributing writers: Ashok, R., Koilparambil, A. J., Cole, W., Westbrook, T., and (Eds.). Cushing, C., & Anantharaman, M. https://www.nytimes.com/Reuters/2019/12/20/business/20reuters-austra-lia-reglator-volkswagen

Rhioux, B., & Lobe, B. (2009). *The case for qualitative analysis* (QCA): *Adding leverage for thick cross-case comparison,* in B. Byrne & C. C. Ragin, (Eds.). *Handbook of cross-case methods.* Sage.

Rhioux, B., & Ragin, C. C. (2009). *Configurational Comparative methods.* Sage.

Robbins, S. P., & Judge, T. A. (2015). *Organizational behavior* (16th ed.). Pearson.

Roberts, A. (2017, April 14). Volkswagen ahead of schedule on buybacks of diesel vehicles. *The Wall Street Journal,* p. B3.

Roberts, G. E. (2015). *Christian scripture and human resource management: Building a path to servant leadership through faith.* Palgrave Macmillan.

Rockoff, J. D., & Silverman, E. (2016, April 26). Pharmaceutical companies buy rival's drugs, then jack up the prices. *The Wall Street Journal.* https://www.wsj.com

Roger, E. (2019, January - February). The many costs of addiction. *Money 48*(1), 5.

Rohmann, C. (1999). *A world of ideas: A dictionary of important theories, concepts, beliefs, and thinkers.* Ballantine.

Ruggiero, R. (2009). *The art of thinking: A guide to critical and creative thought* (9th ed). Pearson Education, Inc.

Russolillo, S., & Bird, M. (2018, December 6). Bots are online – M.B.A. essential. *The Wall Street Journal,* p. B5.

Salovey, P., & Mayer, J. D. (1990). Emotional intelligence. *Imagination, Cognition, and Personality, 9,* 185-211.

Schein, E. H. (2017). *Organizational culture and leadership* (5th ed.). John Wiley & Sons.

Schwandt, T. (2015). *Dictionary of Qualitative research* (4th ed.). Sage.

Schweiger, D. M., & Finger, P. A. (1984). The comparative effectiveness of dialectic inquiry and devil's advocacy. *Strategic Management Journal, 5,* 335-50.

Segal, T. (2018, January 3). Enron Scandal: The fall of a Wall Street darling. *Investopedia.* https://www.investopedia/updates/enron-scandal-summer/

Sekaran, U., & Bougie, R. (2016). *Research methods for business* (7th ed.). Wiley.

Senge, P. M. (1990). *The fifth discipline: The art & practice of the learning organization.* Currency Doubleday

Simon, H. A. (1997). *Administrative behavior: Decision-making processes in administrative organizations* [*Bounded rationality:* An impediment to rational decisions; *Satisficing:* Settling for less than optimal or very beneficial decision options]. (4th ed.). Free Press. (Original work published 1945).

Sitkin, S., & Lind, A. (2018). Six Domains of Leadership. *Duke University Leadership Academy.* https://hr.duke.edu/training/programs/duke-leadership-academy/program-   information/six-domains-leadership

Slater, R. (2003). *29 leadership secrets from Jack Welch; Abridged from Get Better or Get Beaten* [In 2000, this CEO led General Electric to revenues of $129.9 billion, and earnings of $12.7 billion. He embraced company-wide change, listened to employees for good ideas, and challenged managers to be number 1 or 2 in their respective markets] (2nd ed.). McGraw-Hill.

Smith, A. (2009, June 29). Madoff sentenced to 150 years. *CNN Money. CNN Money.com*

Smith, J. L., & Flanagan, W. G. (2006). *Creating competitive advantage: Give your customers a reason to choose you over your competitors.* Currency Doubleday.

Soukhanov, A. H. (Ed.). (1984). *Webster's II new Riverside university dictionary*. Houghton Mifflin.

Stake, R. (1995). *The art of case study research*. Sage.

Steele, A. (2018, February 20). Pandora gets even more personal with its service. *The Wall Street Journal*, p. R10.

Steinbuch, Y. (2017, April 18). Zuckerberg addresses Facebook murder video. *The New York Post*. https://www.nypost.com

Stewart, J. B. (2018, April 19). Punishing Wells Fargo: Just deserts, Or just cruel? [Or beating a dead horse]. *The New York Times*, pp. B1, B4.

Stogdill, R. M., & Coons, A. E. (Eds.). (1957). *Leader behavior: Its description and measurement [Consideration and initiating structure]*. Research Monograph No. 88. Bureau of Business Research. The Ohio State University.

Tau, B., & Seetharaman, D. (2018, March 20). Data blowback pummels Facebook. *The Wall Street Journal*, pp. A1, A6.

TechTarget. (2018). STEM [Science, Technology, Engineering, and Mathematics]. *TechTarget*. https://whatis.techtarget.com/definition/STEM-science-technology-engineering-and-mathematics

Tipgos, M. A. (2002, December). Why management fraud is unstoppable. *The CPA Journal*, *72*(12), 35-43. Infotrac (OneFile) database

Tracy, R. (2018 February 3-4), Fed orders Wells Fargo to change board. *The Wall Street Journal*, p. A1.

Urban, H. (2003). *Life's Greatest Lessons: 20 Things that Matter* (4th ed.). Simon & Schuster.

Verschool, C. C. (2002, December). It isn't enough to just have a code of ethics. *Strategic Finance*, *84*(6), 22-24. ProQuest database

Volberda, H. W., Van Den Bosch, F. A. J., & Hein, C. V. (2013). Management innovation: Management as fertile ground for innovation. *European Management Review*, *10*(1), 1-15.

Volkswagen Accountability Project (VAP). (2018). *Hold Volkswagen accountable*. https://www.holdvwaccountable.com

Volkswagen AG. (2020). *Volkswagen brands*. https://www.volkswagenag.com/en/group.html

VW.com. (2019). *Volkswagen Strategy: Together 2025+*. https://www. vw.com/

Weick, K. E. (1969). *The social psychology of organizing*. Addison-Wesley.

Wells Fargo Bank. (2017, February). *Corporate governance guidelines*. https://www08.wellsfargomedia.com/assets/pdf/about/corporate/governance-guidelines.pdf

Wells Fargo Online. (2019, January 16). *Important information about the government shutdown*. wellsfargo@connect.wellsfargoemail. com

Wells Fargo & Company. (2018, December). *Wells Fargo Business Standards Report: Learning* from the past, transforming for the future. Wells Fargo, N.A.

Werhane, P. H., Hartman, P. L., Archer, C., Englehardt, E. E., & Pritchard, M. S. (2014). *Obstacles to Ethical decision-making: Mental models, milgram and the problem of obedience*. Cambridge University Press.

Wilson, S. (2018). *First, make the beast beautiful: A new journey through anxiety*. Pan MacMillan.

Witman, P. D. (2018). Teaching case "What gets measured, gets managed" the Wells Fargo account opening scandal. *Journal of Information Systems Education, 29*(3), 131-138.

Xiong, Y. (US Army Chaplain, Major). (2019, July 14). Sunday Sermon: *Our strength comes from the Lord*. Kino Gospel Chapel, Fort Huachuca, AZ. US Army.

Yin, R. K. (2018). *Case study research and applications: Design and methods* (6th ed.). Sage.

INDEX A
Terms and Concepts

A-C

D-F

G-I

K-O

P-Q

R-S

T-Z

INDEX B
Organizations

H-N

O-P

Q-U

V-Z